Sexuality

SAGE SERIES ON CLOSE RELATIONSHIPS

Series Editors
Clyde Hendrick, Ph.D., and
Susan S. Hendrick, Ph.D.

Sexuality

Susan Sprecher
Kathleen McKinney

Sage
Series
on Close
Relationships

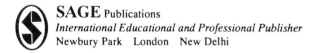

SAGE Publications
International Educational and Professional Publisher
Newbury Park   London   New Delhi

For information address:

SAGE Publications, Inc.
2455 Teller Road
Newbury Park, California 91320

SAGE Publications Ltd.
6 Bonhill Street
London EC2A 4PU
United Kingdom

SAGE Publications India Pvt. Ltd.
M-32 Market
Greater Kailash I
New Delhi 110 048 India

Printed in the United States of America

Library of Congress Cataloging-in-Publication Data

Sprecher, Susan, 1955-
Sexuality / Susan Sprecher, Kathleen McKinney.
  p. cm. —(Sage series on close relationships)
  Includes bibliographical references and index.
  ISBN 0-8039-4290-7. —ISBN 0-8039-4291-5 (pbk.)
  1. Sex. 2. Sex (Psychology) 3. Interpersonal relations.
I. McKinney, Kathleen. II. Title. III. Series.
HQ21.S6246 1993
306.7—dc20   93-6482

93 94 95 96 10 9 8 7 6 5 4 3 2 1

Sage Production Editor: Diane S. Foster

Dedicated to Our Families . . .
Chuck, Abby, and Kate
Bob, Ben, and Claire

Contents

Series Editors' Introduction

When we first began our work on love attitudes more than a decade ago, we did not know what to call our research area. In some ways it represented an extension of earlier work in interpersonal attraction. Most of our scholarly models were psychologists (though sociologists had long been deeply involved in the areas of courtship and marriage), yet we sometimes felt as if our work had no professional "home." That has all changed. Our research not only has a home but also has an extended family, and the family is composed of relationship researchers. During the past decade the discipline of close relationships (also called personal relationships and intimate relationships) has emerged, developed, and flourished.

Two aspects of close relationships research should be noted. The first is its rapid growth, resulting in numerous books, journals, handbooks, book series, and professional organizations. As fast as the field grows, the demand for even more research and knowledge seems to be ever increasing. Questions about close, personal relationships still far exceed answers. The second noteworthy aspect of the new discipline of close relationships is its interdisciplinary nature. The field owes its vitality to scholars from communications, family studies and human development, psychology (clinical, counseling, developmental, social), and sociology, as well as other disciplines such as nursing and social work. It is this interdisciplinary wellspring that gives close relationships research its diversity and richness, qualities that we hope to achieve in the current series.

The **Sage Series on Close Relationships** is designed to acquaint diverse readers with the most up-to-date information about various topics in close relationships theory and research. Each volume in the series covers a particular topic or theme in one area of close relationships. Each book reviews the particular topic area, describes contemporary research in the area (including the authors' own work, where appropriate), and offers some suggestions for interesting research questions and/or real-world applications related to the topic. The volumes are designed to be appropriate for students and professionals in communication, family studies, psychology, sociology, and social work, among others. A basic assumption of the series is that the broad panorama of close relationships can best be portrayed by authors from multiple disciplines, so that the series cannot be "captured" by any single disciplinary bias.

This volume, *Sexuality*, offers a timely, comprehensive, and readable portrait of sexuality in the context of close relationships. Susan Sprecher and Kathleen McKinney have culled the vast literature on sexuality in an attempt to present readers with as complete a picture as possible of current theory and research in the area. The authors guide us from sexuality during the courtship context through sexual satisfaction in long-term relationships and other topics and end with a quietly compelling commentary on sexual coercion in close relationships. In an interesting yet scholarly fashion, the authors document the crucial role of sexuality in so much of our intimate relating.

CLYDE HENDRICK
SUSAN S. HENDRICK
SERIES EDITORS

Preface

This book deals with sexuality in close relationships. Several aspects of sexuality in close relationships are discussed throughout, including sexual attitudes, sexual behaviors, sexual satisfaction, and sexual coercion. Sexuality is not an aspect of all close re- lationships. We focus on one special type of close relationship—the *sexually based primary relationship*. Scanzoni, Polonko, Teachman, and Thompson (1989) defined such relationships as those in which "the persons define sexual exchanges or interdependence as a *legitimate* element/expectation for their type of relationship (whether or not they are currently engaging in sexual activities)" (p. 47). The major types of sexually based relationships are dating, cohabiting, and marital relationships. All three types are discussed in this book. Furthermore, as much as possible, we focus on both heterosexual and homo- sexual relationships. We are limited in our coverage of homosexual relationships, however, due to the dearth of research on this topic.

Sexuality and *close relationships*, as two distinct research areas, are interdisciplinary fields, as is the conjunction of the two (*sexuality in close relationships*). The material reviewed in this book comes from many disciplines. Although we bring our own backgrounds of sociology and social psychology to this book, many other disciplines are represented as well, including psychology, communication, and family studies. This book should be of interest to students, researchers, and practitioners in these disciplines and also may be of interest to a general audience. However, we targeted the book specifically for students and researchers interested in the fields of close relationships and sexuality. Our hope is that this book will stimulate more empirical and theoretical work in the interface between these two fields.

We begin, in Chapter 1, by discussing attitudes about sexuality in close relationships. The focus of this chapter is on attitudes about sexual behavior at different levels of emotional involvement in dating relationships, although research on attitudes about sex in other types of relationships also is summarized. We consider how attitudes have changed over time and the factors that influence how sexually liberal or traditional a person is in his or her views.

In Chapter 2 we provide a brief overview of how a sexual relationship begins, including a discussion of factors that affect initial romantic attraction and sexual attraction, and expand to consider issues such as whether a person's sexual history affects how desirable he or she is for an intimate relationship.

In Chapter 3 we discuss how partners come to have sex for the first time. We consider the decision-making process behind this first time, how partners express their sexual interest and perceive sexual interest in the other, the degree to which partners talk about their respective sexual histories and condom use before having sex, and several other topics concerning the pathway to initial sexual involvement.

The two variables frequently examined in the study of sexuality in more developed close relationships (e.g., marriage) include frequency of sex and sexual satisfaction. These variables are the focus of Chapter 4. We discuss how frequently American couples have sex, what they do while they have sex, how satisfied they are with their sex life, and the factors that influence both frequency and sexual satisfaction.

In Chapter 5 we relate sexual aspects of the relationship to other feelings and behaviors relevant to the relationship. The couple's sex life is not isolated from their general relationship satisfaction, the degree to which and *how* they love each other, any conflicts in their relationship, and the fairness of their relationship. We discuss these associations and present evidence concerning how sex can affect whether the couple breaks up or stays together. The importance of communication to a happy sex life also is discussed.

We turn to a negative side of sexuality in Chapter 6. Although sex in a close relationship is usually consensual, we show that a significant number of females (and also some males) are forced to have sex against their will, either in a dating or even a more committed relationship. We discuss the factors that influence the likelihood of coercive sex and the consequences for the individual victim and for the relationship.

Chapter 7 is our epilogue. We reprise the major themes of the book, make suggestions for future research, and discuss the importance of disseminating scientific knowledge on sexuality in close relationships to the general public.

1

Attitudes About Sexuality in Close Relationships

We love each other, so there's no reason why we shouldn't be making love. (a 16-year-old female interviewed by Rubin, 1990, p. 14)

I found out that sex without marriage is more physically enjoyable than it is mentally. So now I'm saving myself for when I get married. (a 17-year-old female interviewed by Rubin, 1990, p. 64)

If you're looking for a girlfriend, not just some quick and dirty sex, you don't want to get involved with a slut, you know, one of those girls who goes out with more than one guy at a time, or a girl who goes for those one-nighters. You want her to be one of those nice girls, you know, the kind of girl who only has sex with her boyfriend, and she makes sure he's her boyfriend before she does it. (a 17-year-old male interviewed by Rubin, 1990, pp. 70-71)

I've got a couple of good women friends I spend time with, and when I'm not seeing someone and get lonely and horny, if one of them is free too, we get together sexually. (a 37-year-old male interviewed by Rubin, 1990, p. 104)

I think whatever a couple does is their business; it's up to them. There are a few things I won't do, like anal sex . . . . But, my best friend likes it, and if that's what she wants, that's okay. I don't think anyone has the right to judge what people do. It's nobody's business as long as the couple both agree. (a 16-year-old female interviewed by Rubin, 1990, p. 65)

The above quotes reflect *sexual attitudes*, the topic of this chapter. Everyone has a set of sexual attitudes for his or her own behavior and for the behavior of others. These attitudes have a profound influence on whether and how sexual behavior occurs in a particular relationship and to what consequences. These attitudes also affect what we think of our lover, our best friend, our divorced mother, or anyone else when we learn something about his or her sexuality.

In this chapter we deal with many questions about sexual attitudes. We begin with a discussion of sexual attitudes for dating relationships. How are sexual standards about dating relationships defined and measured? What trends in attitudes have occurred over the last 50 years? Do people hold different sexual standards for men and women? What factors influence sexual standards? We also examine the relationship between sexual attitudes and love attitudes. In the second section we discuss standards for sexual behaviors in other types of close relationships; that is, what are people's attitudes toward sexuality in marriage, cohabitation, extramarital, and homosexual relationships?

✒ Sexual Standards for Dating Relationships

Definitions and Types of Standards

Imagine you overhear the following conversation among three young adults who are discussing their attitudes about premarital sex. Whose opinion do you agree with?

Kate says she believes that sexual intercourse should be reserved for marriage because sex is most important for having children and *that*, in her view, should only happen in marriage. Ben accuses her of being too conservative and says that sex before marriage is appropriate if both people want to engage in it for fun. Their friend Claire argues that people should feel free to engage in sexual intercourse before marriage as long as they love their partner.

Several types of sexual standards have been identified. According to one perspective, there are three general orientations toward sexuality: a procreational orientation, a relational orientation, and a recreational orientation (see, for example, the discussion in DeLamater, 1989). Similar to Kate's point of view described above, individuals holding a *procreational orientation* view the primary purpose of sexual intercourse to be that of reproduction—having babies. From a *relational orientation*, sexual intercourse can be a way of expressing love and affection and a way to help increase the emotional intimacy of a relationship, as expressed by Claire. Finally, those like Ben, who hold a *recreational orientation* toward sexual activity, view such behavior primarily as a source of fun and pleasure. These latter two orientations also have been referred to as *person-centered* and *body-centered* sex, respectively (Reiss, 1960).

A similar typology was presented by Peplau, Rubin, and Hill (1977). On the basis of a well-known study of 231 couples that has been called the Boston Dating Couples Study, they described three types of sexual attitudes into which couples could be categorized. First, some of the couples were *sexually traditional.* This view is similar to a procreational perspective in that premarital sex usually is seen as unacceptable. Such abstinence often is based on religious beliefs. The authors illustrated this view with a description of Paul and Peggy, one couple in their study. "Peggy is firmly opposed to premarital sex for herself. Raised a devout Catholic, Peggy believes that intercourse before marriage is wrong . . . and she believes that Paul respects her views" (p. 97). Some of the other couples were placed into the category of *sexually moderate.* These couples disapprove of casual sex but feel that premarital sex is acceptable if the partners are in love. This attitude is similar to the relational perspective described above. Tom and Sandy reflect this group. Tom said, " 'I felt that we shouldn't have sex until our relationship reached a certain point. Sex is something I just can't imagine on a first date.' Just before becoming engaged, Tom and Sandy first had intercourse with each other" (p. 98). Finally, the largest group of couples in the Peplau et al. study were labeled *sexually liberal.* This view is similar to a recreational orientation. For these respondents premarital sex is appropriate as long as both people agree; no emotional involvement is required. This view is illustrated by Diane and Alan. "Diane told

us that she and Alan were not in love when they first had intercourse. Nonetheless, she enjoyed the sex. . . . Diane and Alan view
sex as fun" (p. 98).

Perhaps the most well known typology of premarital sexual standards comes from the work of Reiss (1960, 1967), who defined four
premarital sexual standards. The first standard is *abstinence,* which
is the view that premarital intercourse is wrong for both men and
women. The second standard, the *double standard,* generally gives more
sexual freedom to men than to women. Reiss identified two sub-
types of the double standard. The orthodox (or traditional) double
standard proposes that premarital sex is acceptable for men but that
women must wait for marriage. The transitional (or conditional)
double standard proposes that men may engage in premarital intercourse regardless of the nature of the relationship, whereas women
may only engage in premarital intercourse in the context of a love
relationship. The third standard, *permissiveness with affection,* is the
notion that premarital sex is appropriate for both men and women
in stable, affectionate relationships. Finally the fourth standard, *permissiveness without affection,* makes premarital sex acceptable for
men and women regardless of the emotional quality of the relationship; that is, premarital sex is appropriate if both people consent.

Measurement of Sexual Standards

Assessing people's attitudes or standards about sexual behavior
can be a difficult task. Researchers are concerned about whether they
have good measurement tools and whether the respondents are
being honest. Researchers therefore tend to rely on multiple techniques for measuring sexual attitudes. We briefly discuss the use of
self-administered questions and experimental designs.

Self-Administered Questions and Scales

The most commonly used strategies for measuring individuals'
premarital sexual standards are self-administered single-item questions (e.g., respondents answer a question such as "Do you approve
of sexual intercourse before marriage?") and multiple-item scales.
Sexual standards can be assessed for different referents; that is, we
can ask about general standards (for everyone), standards for cer-

tain groups of people (e.g., women, teenagers), standards for specific others (e.g., a sibling), or standards for the self. The most common distinction is standards for men versus standards for women. This latter issue is discussed in a section on the double standard later in this chapter.

Reiss's (1964) Premarital Sexual Permissiveness Scale (PSP) is one of the most widely used multiple-item scales. Reiss argued that the acceptability of premarital sexual behaviors depends, in part, on the emotional level of the relationship. It was important, therefore, to ask about premarital standards by using more than one question. His original scale included 12 items. Three sexual behaviors (kissing, petting, full sexual relations) were each combined with four levels of emotional or relational involvement (no affection, strong affection, in love, engaged). Respondents were asked to indicate how acceptable (using a 6-point agreement response scale) each behavior is at each affectional level, first with a male as the referent (target) and second with a female referent. Two example items are "I believe that petting is acceptable for the male when he is engaged" and "I believe that full sexual relations is acceptable for the female when she is in love."

Recently Reiss (1989) revised his original scale, combining the separate questions on males and females into one by eliminating the gender reference (the items do not include *she* or *he*) and changing the affectional levels to (a) without much affection, (b) moderate affection, (c) strong affection, and (d) love relationship. For example, "I believe that premarital intercourse is acceptable if one is in a love relationship."

Other self-administered scales have been developed to measure sexual standards. We, along with two colleagues (Sprecher, McKinney, Walsh, & Anderson, 1988), presented a revision of the original Reiss PSP, taking into account some of the criticisms that scale has received. The original Reiss scale has been criticized for using outdated terms (e.g., *full sexual relations*), not including some common forms of sexual behavior (e.g., oral-genital sex), and using relational categories that are somewhat ambiguous and not mutually exclusive (e.g., in love, engaged) (Clayton & Bokemeier, 1980; Hampe & Ruppel, 1974; Sprecher et al., 1988). We dealt with all of these concerns in our revision of the scale by asking about the acceptability

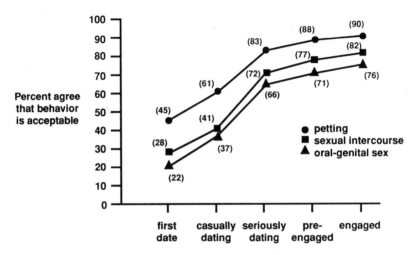

Figure 1.1. Acceptance of Sexual Activity by Relationship Stages (From Sprecher, McKinney, Walsh, & Anderson, 1989)

of petting, sexual intercourse, and oral-genital sex in each of the following relationship stages: first date, casually dating, seriously dating, preengaged, and engaged. Some of our results are summarized in Figure 1.1. For example, we found that petting was the sexual behavior accepted by the largest percentage of subjects, then sexual intercourse, and finally oral-genital sex. Furthermore subjects were more accepting of all three types of sexual behavior at more committed relationship stages than at less committed stages.

Another measure of sexual attitudes was created by Hendrick and Hendrick (1987c), called the Sexual Attitudes Scale (SAS). The SAS was designed to be a general, multidimensional measure of sexual attitudes. It contains four subscales, including a subscale measuring sexual permissiveness. The authors explained why they developed such a scale: "It seems clear that there are several important types of sexual attitudes; such attitudes are multidimensional. In order to capture this range, and to assess sexual permissiveness at all periods of life (not just before marriage), we devised the Sexual Attitudes Scale" (p. 120). Below are the subscale names and example items for each scale.

1. Permissiveness (tolerance and acceptance of sexual activity): "Casual sex is acceptable"; "Extensive premarital experience is all right."
2. Sexual Practices (engaging in types of sexually related behaviors): "A man should share responsibility for birth control"; "Masturbation is all right."
3. Communion (the extent to which sexuality is viewed as a means for merging with the partner): "Sex gets better as a relationship progresses"; "Sex is a very important part of life."
4. Instrumentality (the extent to which sex is seen as body focused vs. person focused): "Sex is primarily physical"; "The main purpose of sex is to enjoy oneself."

Hendrick and Hendrick (1992) reported that both males and females most strongly endorse sexual communion and sexual practices. In addition, males score higher than females on both the permissiveness and instrumentality subscales. They found no differences, however, between men and women on communion or sexual practices.

Many other scales and indices are used to assess sexual standards or attitudes, including the Fisher, White, Byrne, and Kelley (1988) Sexual Opinion Survey; the Sexual Double Standard Scale, by Muehlenhard and Quackenbush (1988); Gangestad and Simpson's (1990) Sociosexual Orientation Inventory (SOI); and measures by Laner, Laner, and Palmer (1978), Mahoney (1980), and Mercer and Kohn (1979).

The Experimental Approach

Some researchers use an experimental approach to measure sexual attitudes. In these experiments subjects are given information (usually in written form) about a hypothetical person (target) and then are asked to make judgments or evaluations of this person, based on the information received. The information focuses on the target person's sexual behavior and/or attitudes. Some subjects receive information describing the person as sexually permissive, and others receive information describing the person as sexually conservative. A condition in which the person is described as moderately permissive also may be included. For example, the subjects may be told that this person had several sexual partners (or none) or had sex for the first time in a casual relationship (or a committed one). This is a less direct method of measuring sexual standards than overtly asking people about their sexual standards as in the self-administered items and scales described above. It is assumed that the judgments subjects make reflect the sexual attitudes or standards they hold.

BOX 1.1

Example Experimental Material

1. Gender: X_ male ___ female
2. At what age did you first have sexual intercourse?   16
3. How old was your partner at the time of this experience?   16
4. Please describe your relationship at the time of your first intercourse.

"It was a steady relationship; we had been dating almost one year."

Please rate the student above on the following adjective pairs.

submissive					dominant	
1	2	3	4	5	6	7
traditional					liberal	
1	2	3	4	5	6	7
unintelligent					intelligent	
1	2	3	4	5	6	7
promiscuous					not promiscuous	
1	2	3	4	5	6	7

Box 1.1 contains an example of some target information (subjects were told that the page was from a questionnaire filled out by another student) and four dependent variables, similar to information given subjects in one of our studies (Sprecher, McKinney, & Orbuch, 1987). We manipulated information about the gender of the student, the student's age at first intercourse, and the type of relationship the student had with the partner at first intercourse. Imagine you were asked to read this scenario and respond to these questions. How would you rate this person on the items listed? Results of studies such as these are discussed in the following sections of this chapter.

In conclusion, the Reiss PSP or a version of that scale is still one of the most commonly used scales to assess premarital sexual standards. This and other scales are used most often in survey studies of college students or other young adults. In addition, some researchers use paper-and-pencil experiments to tap people's views of the acceptability of sexual behavior in dating relationships.

Changes in Sexual Standards Over Time

"Attitudes toward female sexuality in general, and premarital sexuality in particular, have become increasingly permissive in the United States during the twentieth century" (Reiss & Lee, 1988, p. 157). In this section we discuss trends over time periods in sexual standards for dating relationships. Then we look at the current status of the double standard.

Sexual Standards in Different Eras

Researchers agree that prior to the 1960s, abstinence and the traditional double standard were the most common sexual standards for dating relationships held by young adults (e.g., Darling, Kallen, & Van Dusen, 1984; Ehrmann, 1959; Kaats & Davis, 1970; Reiss, 1967); that is, the majority of adults believed that premarital sexual intercourse either was unacceptable for both men and women or was acceptable for men but not for women.

During the 1960s and 1970s, often considered to be the era of the sexual revolution, sexual standards for dating relationships became more permissive. For example, Singh (1980) analyzed data from a national probability sample of adults for 5 years between 1972 and 1978. Singh reported a gradual decrease over time in the percentage of respondents who said that premarital sex is always wrong. In a study of changing sexual norms on a college campus between 1963 and 1978, Sherwin and Corbett (1985) found increased liberalism in these norms over that time period and especially a movement toward a norm of permissiveness with affection. Greeley (1991) analyzed data from the General Social Survey, a longitudinal study of representative samples of American adults, and concluded that in 1972 "26 percent thought that premarital sex was not wrong at all. In 1988 that had risen to 40 percent—the change happening in the first ten years and the rate being essentially constant since then" (p. 219). Other trend or cohort longitudinal studies by Mahoney (1978); Ferrell, Tolone, and Walsh (1977); King, Balswick, and Robinson (1977); and Robinson and Jedlicka (1982) all found evidence for a decrease in the traditional double standard and an increase in more permissive premarital standards for men and women during the 1970s. Yet not all of the recent research completely supports this conclusion. Lawrance, Rubinson, and O'Rourke (1984) reported support for stable, rather than increasingly permissive, premarital sexual attitudes across three time periods—1972, 1977, and 1982.

Research on sexual standards from the late 1970s/early 1980s through the late 1980s is also not entirely consistent. Most researchers argue that this era is characterized by a continued liberalization of sexual standards, with the standards of permissiveness either with or without affection most prevalent, and the traditional double standard less prevalent (e.g., Darling et al., 1984; Robinson & Jedlicka, 1982; Walsh, 1989). In a comparison of sexual standards for dating relationships of college students at one Midwestern college in 1982 and 1988, Bishop and Lipsitz (1991) found that both men and women students in the 1988 sample were significantly more liberal in attitudes about premarital intercourse than were the students in the 1982 sample. Robinson, Ziss, Ganza, and Katz (1991) described data collected from college students over a period of 20 years (1965 to 1985). From the students' responses to a 5-item premarital attitude scale, the researchers concluded that a consistent decrease in negative attitudes about premarital intercourse occurred. When looking at promiscuity (how immoral or sinful it is to have many partners), however, they found that a larger percentage of male and female respondents in the 1980s than in the 1970s viewed promiscuity negatively. Across the years of the study, the attitudes toward promiscuity in females were more negative than the attitudes toward promiscuity in males (a double standard).

Many possible reasons have been proposed for the probable trend away from more conservative standards toward greater permissiveness. In particular this trend is related to other changes in society since World War II, such as technological innovations that decrease the risk of pregnancy and/or simplify birth control (e.g., the pill), increasing political liberalism, the women's movement, and the influence of sexual messages in the mass media (King et al., 1977; Walsh, 1989). We argue that some of what appears to be inconsistent results (a recent trend toward more conservative standards) actually reflects a new transition period in sexual standards for dating relationships; that is, in the early to mid-1980s, AIDS began to receive mass media attention. Due to time lags in attitudinal change and in research studies of such change, we have only begun to see hints of this trend in the last few years—the late 1980s to early 1990s. (See also Carroll, 1988, for a discussion of AIDS and social change.)

What Has Happened to the Double Standard?

DeLamater and MacCorquodale (1979) concluded from their survey study of young adults, "The double standard has virtually disappeared" (p. 229). Yet Rubin (1990), after surveying and interviewing American adults, wrote, "Ideally, the norm calling for serial monogamy applies to all regardless of gender. . . . In the real world, the double standard of sexuality that has for so long defined our sexual consciousness has been wounded, but is not yet dead" (p. 69). What is the status of the double standard? Do people hold different premarital sexual standards for men versus those for women?

Most recent survey research has indicated a decrease, if not a disappearance, of the traditional double standard in which premarital sex is seen as acceptable for men but not for women (e.g., DeLamater & MacCorquodale, 1979; Spreadbury, 1982). In two other studies, using a revision of the Reiss Premarital Sexual Permissiveness Scale, Sprecher et al. (1988) and Sprecher (1989a) also failed to find evidence for a double standard. In these studies, participants who completed the sexual permissiveness scale for a male did not respond differently from participants who completed the scale for a female.

In the Boston Dating Couples Study, Peplau et al. (1977) found that "most students rejected a double standard of sexual conduct. . . . When students held different attitudes for the behavior of men and women, however, they almost always took a more permissive attitude towards men" (pp. 90-91). For example, both men and women saw casual sex as more acceptable for men than for women.

Muehlenhard and Quackenbush (1988), using their Sexual Double Standard Scale, found that male and female college students still hold this standard to a certain degree. Example items from their scale include "It's worse for a woman to sleep around than it is for a man" and "I kind of feel sorry for a 21-year-old man who is still a virgin."

In several studies (Garcia, 1983; Istvan & Griffitt, 1980; Jacoby & Williams, 1985; Mark & Miller, 1986) experimental designs were used to assess the existence of a double standard. None of these studies found support for the double standard. Female target persons were not judged significantly more negatively for the same sexual behavior than were male target persons. As an exception, Sprecher, McKinney, and Orbuch (1987) found that a young female was judged more negatively than a young male for having sexual intercourse the first time in a casual relationship. This is an example of a conditional double standard in which the double standard operates only under certain circumstances (e.g., in a casual relationship).

These conflicting results about the status of the double standard are probably due, in part, to differences in samples and methodologies across the studies. We can conclude cautiously that the traditional double standard has decreased or disappeared in young American adults but that conditional double standards still exist.

Influences on Sexual Standards Today

What types of variables affect people's sexual standards and attitudes? In this section we summarize some of the major findings on how cultural, subcultural, group, and individual factors influence people's sexual standards for dating relationships.

Cultural Influences

The sexual values that exist at the cultural level and that are supported by institutions in society, such as schools, family, and religion, will affect the sexual attitudes and norms held by groups and individuals within that society. Research suggests that young adults in Scandinavian countries, some Western European countries, and the United States tend to accept a "permissiveness with affection" standard. In addition, these groups are more liberal or permissive in terms of their sexual standards toward dating relationships than Asian, Mexican, and Middle Eastern young people (e.g., Alzate, 1984; Iwawaki & Eysenck, 1978; LaBeff & Dodder, 1982; Shapurian & Hojat, 1985; Werebe & Reinert, 1983).

Subcultural Influences

Subcultural membership also influences sexual standards. Research generally supports the conclusion that blacks hold more permissive premarital sexual standards than do whites (e.g., Harrison, Bennett, Globetti, & Alsikafi, 1974; Staples, 1978; Weinberg & Williams, 1988). White college students, however, were found to be more permissive than another minority group—Mexican American college students (Hendrick & Hendrick, 1987a; Padilla & O'Grady, 1987).

Findings on the relationship between social class and premarital sexual permissiveness have been inconsistent, with some studies showing no differences in standards by class (e.g., Brown, 1985; DeLamater & MacCorquodale, 1979; McCabe & Collins, 1983; Padilla & O'Grady, 1987; Reiss, 1967) and others showing that lower class respondents are more permissive than middle or upper class respondents (e.g., Kantner & Zelnick, 1972).

Furthermore, studies indicate that greater religiosity or more frequent attendance at religious events is associated with more restrictive or conservative premarital sexual standards (e.g., DeLamater & MacCorquodale, 1979; Hendrick & Hendrick, 1987a; McCabe & Collins, 1983).

The Influence of Family and Friends

Research generally shows that peer standards have a stronger impact on respondents' standards than do parental standards (DeLamater & MacCorquodale, 1979; Reiss, 1967). Parental standards tend to have a conservative effect on a young adult's level of permissiveness, whereas peer standards tend to have a liberalizing effect (DeLamater & MacCorquodale, 1979; Libby, Gray, & White, 1978; Walsh, 1989).

The Influences of Individual Characteristics

Numerous survey and experimental studies show that males are more permissive than females, especially in the context of casual relationships (e.g., Carroll, Volk, & Hyde, 1985; Hendrick, Hendrick, Slapion-Foote, & Foote, 1985; Lawrance, Rubinson, & O'Rourke, 1984; McCabe, 1987; Mercer & Kohn, 1979; Roche, 1986; Smith, Resick, & Kilpatrick, 1980; Sprecher, 1989a).

Age also has been shown to be related to premarital standards. Most research indicates that older college-age respondents have more permissive standards than younger college-age respondents (e.g., DeLamater & MacCorquodale, 1979; Dignan & Anspaugh, 1978; Ferrell et al., 1977; McCabe & Collins, 1983; Yalom, Brewster, & Estler, 1981). Older adults, however, are less permissive than young adults (Reiss, 1967).

Recent research has compared heterosexuals and homosexuals in their attitudes about sexuality. Adler, Hendrick, and Hendrick (1986) conducted a comparison of male homosexuals and heterosexuals on sexual attitudes and found that the homosexuals were more permissive than the heterosexuals on the permissiveness subscale of the Sexual Attitudes Scale.

Finally, several researchers have considered how other individual characteristics (personality traits, attitudes) affect premarital sexual standards. For example, the following factors have been associated with more permissive sexual standards toward dating relationships (e.g., DeLamater & MacCorquodale, 1979; Hendrick & Hendrick, 1987b; Mercer & Kohn, 1979; Snyder, Simpson, & Gangestad, 1986):

1. the perception of the self as desirable to others
2. high self-esteem
3. an internal locus of control (believing that the self controls outcomes in life)
4. high self-monitoring (altering one's behavior according to the cues of the situation and audience)
5. experience seeking (wanting to try new things)
6. susceptibility to boredom
7. egalitarian or less traditional sex roles
8. physical attractiveness (for women only)

9. political and social liberalism
10. lower sex guilt (feeling less guilty, embarrassed, negative about sexuality)

The Relationship Between Love Attitudes and Sexual Attitudes

How are people's feelings about love related to their feelings about sex? Here is the view of one husband: "It's always been my belief that sex and love are two different things. For a man, sex is a physical thing and it can be as impersonal and as casual as shaking somebody's hand or eating a sandwich" (Blumstein & Schwartz, 1983, p. 257). Blumstein and Schwartz (1983), in their large-scale survey study, compared different subgroups in their sample in terms of what percentages of people accept sex without love. More men approved of sex without love than did women in married, cohabiting, and homosexual couples. Cohabitors and homosexuals were more accepting of sex without love than were married people.

Several studies have assessed the relationship between degree of permissiveness of sexual standards and some measure of love attitudes, beliefs, or experiences. For example, Weis, Slosnerick, Cate, and Sollie (1986) created a measure of the extent to which people associate sex, love, and marriage (the SLM scale). Example items on this scale include "A man can't have a satisfactory sex life without being in love with his partner" and "Sexual intercourse is best when enjoyed for its own sake, rather than for the purpose of proving or expressing love." Weis et al. found that those with low SLM scores (less association among sex, love, and marriage) were significantly more permissive in their sexual attitudes about dating relationships. They did not find a difference between males and females on the SLM scale.

Hendrick and Hendrick (1987a, 1987c, 1988) have done extensive research on the relationship between love attitudes and sexual attitudes. They noted, "The study of love and sexuality as companion variables is one of our goals in close relationship research, because it is apparent to us that trying to separate love from sexuality is like trying to separate fraternal twins: they are certainly not identical, but, nevertheless, they are strongly bonded" (1987a, p. 282). The Hendricks have developed scales to measure both sexual attitudes (their Sexual Attitudes Scale was discussed earlier in this chapter) and love attitudes. Their Love Attitudes Scale is based on a typology of love styles (Lee, 1973). The six love styles and an example item for each is given below (from Hendrick & Hendrick, 1987c, p. 285):

1. *Eros (romantic, passionate love):* "I feel that my lover and I are meant for each other."
2. *Ludus (game-playing love):* "I enjoy playing the 'game of love' with a number of different partners."
3. *Storge (friendship love):* "The best kind of love grows out of a long friendship."
4. *Pragma (logical, practical love):* "It is best to love someone with a similar background."
5. *Mania (possessive, dependent love):* "When my lover doesn't pay attention to me, I feel sick all over."
6. *Agape (selfless love):* "I would rather suffer myself than let my lover suffer."

Hendrick and Hendrick (1987c) found that the more times an individual reported that he or she had been in love, the more permissive were his or her standards. Yet being in love currently was associated with less permissive standards. In their study, permissiveness also was related to different styles of love. More specifically, greater permissiveness was associated with ludus (gamelike love), and less permissiveness was associated with agape (selfless, giving love), storge (platonic or friendship love), and pragma (practical love). In a related study Hendrick and Hendrick (1988) found that respondents who were in love were less permissive and less instrumental than respondents not in love. They stated, "Love and sexuality are strongly linked to each other and to both the physical and spiritual aspects of the human condition. For romantic personal relationships, sexual love and loving sexuality may well represent intimacy at its best" (Hendrick & Hendrick, 1987c, p. 293).

In summary, numerous characteristics of the individual and his or her groups and culture have been found to relate to the individual's sexual standards for dating relationships. Some of the most consistent results include that males, older young adults, blacks, less religious individuals, individuals with more positive self-images and more egalitarian attitudes, and individuals with peers who hold more permissive standards tend to be more permissive.

ᴥ Sexual Attitudes About Other Types of Close Relationships

Attitudes About Sex in Marriage

Not much research exists on attitudes and standards about marital sexuality. This lack of research is probably because it is implicitly assumed that everyone approves of sex in marriage, and there is a separate literature (see section below) on attitudes about extramarital sex. What research does exist focuses on the role of sexuality in marriage and changes in marital sexuality for women. Reiss and Lee (1988) summarized these attitudes about marital sex in the following way: "Norms regarding marital sexuality have become increasingly liberal, in terms of sexual experimentation, the use of nontraditional positions, and, perhaps most importantly, the increasing emphasis on the sexual satisfaction of wives as well as husbands" (pp. 252-253).

One way to look at attitudes about sexuality in marriage is to analyze the content of marriage manuals. One such analysis was conducted by Weinberg, Swensson, and Hammersmith (1983). These researchers studied the contents of 49 sex and marriage manuals published in the United States between 1950 and 1980. They concluded that the manuals present one of three models of female sexuality. The first model is *different and unequal* and was found in manuals from the 1950 to 1973 era. Although women were encouraged to enjoy sex, this model still assumed important gender differences in sexuality, including women needing to combine love with sex more than do men, and women needing a skillful partner to awaken their sex drive. The second model of female sexuality found by these authors is *humanistic sexuality*. This model dominated the manuals published between 1973 and 1974. The main characteristic of this model is that female sexuality is removed from the institution of marriage; that is, it is acknowledged that women may engage in sexual behaviors outside of a marital relationship. Female sexuality in these manuals still involves the key element of a loving relationship but also allows for experimentation and exploration. Finally, Weinberg et al. (1983) found evidence for a third model of female sexuality, *sexual autonomy*. This model is common in the manuals from 1975 to 1980. Women were portrayed as sexually independent and in charge of their own sexuality.

It is clear from the limited research cited above that there are different views or attitudes about marital sexuality, especially for the role of female sexuality in marriage.

Attitudes About Extramarital and Extradyadic Sex

A considerable amount of research exists on *normative attitudes* toward extramarital sexuality—that is, attitudes about the acceptability of extramarital sex for people in general. These studies assess the extent to which, and under what circumstances, people see such behavior as acceptable, moral, appropriate, or justified. For example, Reiss (e.g., Reiss & Lee, 1988) created the Extramarital Sexual Permissiveness Scale, which assesses people's attitudes toward extramarital intercourse for husbands or wives under various conditions (e.g., a happy vs. an unhappy marriage). An example item from that scale is: "A husband is in a happy marriage. In the extramarital relationship love is emphasized and this type of relationship is approved of by his mate. Do you find this extramarital relationship acceptable?"

A second area of research on extramarital standards looks at *personal standards*, or standards for the self, such as those illustrated in Box 1.2 by the following quotes.

BOX 1.2

Diane: "We've never spoken about cheating, but neither of us believe in it. I don't think I'd ever forgive him. I don't think I'd be able to. I don't know. I haven't met up with that situation."

Bruce (Diane's husband of five years): "Sure we have an understanding. It's 'You do what you want. Never go back to the same one.' See, that's where it's going to screw your mind up, to go back the second time to the same person." (as cited in Blumstein & Schwartz, 1983, pp. 286-287)

Personal standards can be measured by a self-permissiveness version of the Reiss scale discussed above (see Davis, 1987). An alternative is to present individuals with a story that could involve their engaging in extramarital sex and to ask them their feelings about sexual behavior in the situation depicted in the story (see Johnson, 1970).

Results of the research on both normative and personal standards toward extramarital sexuality indicate that, overall, most people in Western cultures disapprove of extramarital sexuality in general and for the self (e.g., Glenn & Weaver, 1979; Klemmack & Roff, 1980; Lawson & Samson, 1988; Reiss, Anderson, & Sponaugle, 1980; Singh, Walton, & Williams, 1976). For example, from 1980 national data (Davis, 1980), 4% of American adults felt that extramarital sex was never wrong, and 70% felt that it was always wrong. From responses to the General Social Survey in 1988 (Greeley, 1991), 86% of American adults said that marital infidelity (sexual relations with someone other than the marriage partner) was always wrong or almost always wrong.

We have limited information on attitudes toward other extradyadic relationships (sexual relationships outside of committed but nonmarital relationships). As part of a larger study of homosexual and heterosexual couples, Kurdek (1991b) compared the attitudes toward sexual fidelity of several subgroups. He reported that gay couples value fidelity significantly less than lesbian or heterosexual couples. Peplau and Cochran (1981) reported that sexual exclusivity in relationships was rated as more important by heterosexuals than by a matched group of homosexuals. However, most homosexuals, like heterosexuals, do value or prefer steady, love relationships (Bell & Weinberg, 1978; Peplau & Gordon, 1983).

Men, compared to women, may be more accepting of cheating on a partner in a dating relationship than in a marriage. In a study comparing attitudes about extramarital and extradating sexual relationships, Margolin (1989) found that female subjects felt that sexual infidelity was equally unacceptable in both types of relationships, whereas male subjects felt that sexual infidelity in a dating relationship was less unacceptable than in a marriage relationship. Furthermore, both male and female subjects were less accepting of sexual infidelity by members of the opposite sex than by members of their own sex.

Other studies assess what factors relate to or predict extramarital attitudes. In a recent literature review, Sponaugle (1989) reported that greater acceptance of extramarital sexuality is related to being male, holding more permissive premarital standards, lower marital satisfaction and marital sexual satisfaction, higher educational attainment, lower religiosity, perceived opportunity for extramarital activity, greater gender equality, higher liberalism, and being unmarried. In an earlier review, Thompson (1983) argued that premarital sexual standards are the best predictor of extramarital sexual standards, probably because both premarital and extramarital permissiveness are influenced by some of the same factors, such as gender, race, and general liberalism. Reiss et al. (1980), from an analysis of survey data from representative samples of adults obtained by the National Opinion Research Center (NORC), also found that premarital sexual permissiveness, along with marital satisfaction, was a key predictor of extramarital permissiveness.

In conclusion, the majority of men and women in Western societies disapprove of extramarital sexuality. The degree of extramarital permissiveness, however, is influenced by many factors, including opportunity, demographic factors, sex roles, and premarital sexual permissiveness.

Attitudes About Cohabitation

The limited research on attitudes about cohabitation does not contain questions asking directly about sexual behavior. Rather the questions ask about cohabitation itself, which is a type of living arrangement that implies sexual activity outside of marriage.

Research shows that college-age adults tend to be accepting of cohabitation under most circumstances. For example, Bower and Christopher (1977) found that college students generally were approving of cohabitation as long as no children were involved and the couple was monogamous. Sixty percent of these students felt that cohabitation was appropriate in order to try out a relationship.

Adults from the general population, however, appear to express more concerns or reservations, though this expression depends on the year of the study, the sample, and the way the attitude question is phrased. In a late 1970s poll of American adults (McClosky & Brill,

1983), 46% of the sample said living together was morally wrong. Wiersma (1983) studied a probability sample of American adults who were cohabiting, and 72% of this group said their relatives and friends had some concerns about their cohabitation relationship. Finally, in a more recent study analyzing data from the National Survey of Families and Households (Sweet, Bumpass, & Call, 1988), respondents who were unmarried and younger than 36 years old were asked about their attitudes toward cohabitation. Of these respondents, 35% indicated a definite desire to live with someone without being married to find out whether they would be compatible for marriage, and 51% said it would be all right for them to do so.

Attitudes About Homosexual Relationships

Heterosexuals have different perceptions of homosexual compared to heterosexual relationships. For example, Testa, Kinder, and Ironson (1987) found that heterosexuals perceived gay and lesbian couples, as compared to heterosexual couples, to be less in love and less satisfied with their relationship.

Research also has explored general attitudes toward homosexual behavior. Below is an example of a question on sexual standards about homosexual relationships from the General Social Survey, along with the percentage of respondents who chose each response (Davis & Smith, 1987):

Are sexual relations between two adults of the same sex:
Always wrong (75%)
Almost always wrong (4%)
Wrong only sometimes (7%)
Not wrong at all (12%)

Most of the research on attitudes about homosexuals or homosexuality uses the concept of homophobia. *Homophobia* usually refers to negative and/or fearful attitudes about homosexuals or homosexuality. Many measures and scales of homophobia exist (e.g., Herek, 1984; Hudson & Ricketts, 1980; Kite & Deaux, 1986; Millham, San Miguel, & Kellogg, 1976; Seltzer, 1992). Below are some example items from the scale by Kite and Deaux (1986):

"I would not mind having homosexual friends."
"Gays dislike members of the opposite sex."
"I would look for a new place to live if I found out my roommate was gay."
"I would not be afraid for my child to have a homosexual teacher."

According to recent research, being male, older, less educated, traditional, religiously conservative, single, and from a rural area are all associated with greater homophobia (e.g., Britton, 1990; Seltzer, 1992). Kurdek (1988) found similar correlates with negative homosexual attitudes and also reported that although women are less homophobic than men, the correlates of homophobia are similar for both genders.

In conclusion, most heterosexuals hold negative attitudes toward sexual behavior in homosexual couples. In addition, homophobia is a common response to homosexuality and is associated with several demographic variables.

✒ Summary

The purpose of this chapter was to summarize and discuss the area of sexual attitudes for close relationships. We attempted to provide a basic overview of the types of premarital sexual standards that exist, how they are measured, changes in those standards over the last few decades, and the factors that affect the standards that people hold. In addition, we briefly discussed sexual standards and attitudes for other types of close relationships. The role of close relationships in the research on sexual attitudes was covered throughout the chapter. Relationship stage or status is included in definitions and measurement of *sexual standards* and affects the acceptance of sexual behavior. Research shows that sexual attitudes can influence sexual behavior. Sexual behavior in close relationships is discussed in later chapters of this book.

2

The Beginning of the Sexual Relationship

Before we discuss what couples do in their sex life and the effect of sex on other aspects of the close relationship (to be discussed in succeeding chapters), we examine first how close relationships begin. How and where do romantic partners meet and begin dating? Why are some people attracted to each other, whereas others are not? Are the predictors of sexual attraction the same as predictors of romantic attraction? Does a partner's sexual past affect our attraction for him or her? These are some of the questions addressed in this chapter.

❧ The Stages of Coming Together

Several stages are involved in the beginning of the dating or romantic relationship. We focus on the stages of (a) seeing each other for the first time, (b) meeting, and (c) going on a first date.

First Seeing

Before a relationship can begin between two people, they must be aware of each other. This awareness may occur only seconds before the first face-to-face interaction, or it may occur days, weeks, or even months before (e.g., Marwell, McKinney, Sprecher, DeLamater, & Smith, 1982). Two people may both become aware of each other at the same time, or the awareness may be unilateral; that is, one person may notice the other but not be noticed yet in return (e.g., Levinger & Snoek, 1972).

The setting in which first awareness occurs may influence how quickly and easily the relationship progresses to a first meeting. Murstein (1970, 1986) distinguished between closed fields and open fields as settings in which first awareness occurs and relationships begin. A *closed field* is characterized by the presence of a small number of people who are all likely to interact. Small college classes or seminars, some living residences (e.g., a small apartment complex), and some work settings (e.g., the staff at a fast-food restaurant) are examples of closed fields. In the closed field, both awareness and interaction among the participants are virtually guaranteed, and both are likely to occur almost simultaneously. In contrast, an *open field* contains too many people to allow for attention to and interaction with everyone. Examples of open fields include large dances, singles bars, videodating services, and public locations such as shopping malls. Initial awareness may occur in an open field, but a face-to-face meeting may not occur until some time later. Because the open field does not have structured interaction among all participants, people need to plan and scheme for how they will attempt to meet someone they notice and find attractive in such a setting.

First Meeting

Consider the following first meeting that occurred between a man and a woman at a party:

Shelley first noticed him over by the keg, talking to her friend Danny. He was in profile and had the body of a runner; she wandered over to talk to one of her girlfriends so that she could see his face. She liked the way his laugh dissolved slowly into a smile and decided that she would go over to the keg and get Danny to introduce them. By the time she made her way through the party crowd, Danny had gone, so as she approached the keg, she glanced at him briefly and licked her lips. She flicked her hair back over her shoulder with her hand, smiled more directly at the stranger, and reached for the pump. He smiled back and said, "Let me give you a hand with that." She thanked him, and after her plastic cup was filled, he said, "What's your name, anyway?" (from Allgeier & Royster, 1991, p. 133)

According to data collected in a study by Berger (1987b) on the initiation of dating relationships, people use three general techniques to meet another person in an open field, such as a large party. One way is to *introduce themselves,* which may be preceded by observation, mutual gaze, and/or a casual remark. The second way is to give nonverbal cues and *wait for the other to introduce him- or herself.* The third way is to *have a friend make the introduction.* With a sample of university students, Berger (1987b) found that the first strategy, which is the most direct one, was more characteristic of males, whereas the other two strategies were more characteristic of females. (Note that Shelley, in the scenario above, first planned to get a friend to make an introduction and when that became impossible, she "flipped her hair back" and smiled at the man.) Other research also shows that women are subtle and indirect in their early initiation behaviors, whereas men are more direct and bold. For example, Muehlenhard and Dorsey (1987) found that men are more likely than women to telephone someone they want to date, ask for a phone number, initiate a conversation, and engage in other behaviors that demonstrate romantic interest.

When one person approaches another to say hello for the first time, he or she must plan what to say first. Three types of *opening lines* have been identified (Kleinke, Meeker, & Staneski, 1986): cute-flippant, innocuous, and direct. Examples of the three types of opening lines in general situations are "Your place or mine?" (cute-flippant), "Have you seen any good movies lately?" (innocuous), and "I'm sort of shy, but I'd like to get to know you" (direct). In survey studies, Kleinke et al. (1986) found that both men and women rated cute-flippant opening lines as least desirable. They also found that women disliked cute-flippant lines more than men did but liked innocuous lines to a greater degree. Cunningham (1989) found similar results in a field study conducted in suburban Chicago bars. He concluded that "a male who tries to be devastatingly clever with a female may simply devastate his chances of success" (p. 40).

The other way to meet someone is via an introduction from a friend or other third party. Research conducted with samples of college students, high school students, and older single adults shows that about one-third to one-half of relationships begin through an introduction made by another person (e.g., Knox & Wilson, 1981; Marwell et al., 1982; Parks & Eggert, 1991; Simenauer & Carroll, 1982). Some introductions are happenstance, but others are carefully orchestrated. A matchmaking friend may make the introduction, or one of the potential partners may plan the introduction as a way to meet the other potential partner (Berger, 1987b; Marwell et al., 1982). When two people meet through a mutual friend, there may be fewer barriers to continued interaction because it may be assumed that the friend, through the interaction, is saying, "Both of you are okay and therefore you may like each other." In other words, some of the uncertainty about the other, which can be unpleasant (Berger, 1987a), can be reduced through the friend's introduction. Introductions may be especially important for first meetings between homosexual individuals, who want to know whether the other is gay or lesbian.

Where do couples meet for the first time? Research shows that relationships, particularly for younger adults, are more likely to begin in a party situation than in any other type of setting. Other common places for meeting dates include classes, work, bars or nightclubs, and settings centered around hobbies or sports (e.g., Knox & Wilson, 1981; Marwell et al., 1982; Simenauer & Carroll, 1982).

Although most people meet their dates in traditional ways (such as through friends and at parties), some people use commercial ways of meeting. These include personal ads, singles clubs, and videodating services. Woll and Cozby (1987) identified five barriers to the initiation of romantic relationships that might lead people to use more nontraditional ways of meeting potential dating partners. These barriers are shyness, lack of access to a pool of eligible partners, lack of time to initiate relationships in more traditional ways, having a stigma (e.g, overweight, especially tall), or having special needs (e.g., certain sexual needs or preferences).

The First Date

Many barriers need to be overcome in going beyond a first meeting to a first date, including shyness, fear of rejection, and traditional sex role norms that dictate that females are not supposed to initiate courtship behaviors (Sprecher & McKinney, 1987). For most people, however, a strong desire for a relationship overcomes any barriers that may be experienced. Both men and women contribute to the initiation of first dates, although in different ways. Berger (1987b) found that males are more likely to engage in direct steps, such as asking for the other's phone number and asking the other out. Women are more likely to engage in indirect strategies, such as hinting and arranging to "bump into" the other. Although many women have said they have asked a man out and many men have said they have been asked out, men ask out at a greater frequency (e.g., Berger, 1987b; Green & Sandos, 1983; Kelley, Pilchowicz, & Byrne, 1981). Furthermore, research suggests that female-initiated relationships do not last as long as male-initiated ones (e.g., Kelley et al., 1981).

Male initiation and dominance continue on the first date. Rose and Frieze (1989) asked university students to list the actions a woman and a man are likely to take as they prepare for a first date, meet the other person, spend time during the date, and end the date. Men, to a greater degree than women, were expected to be the initiators and planners. Men were expected to ask for the date, decide what to do, pay for the activities of the date, initiate physical contact, and ask for another date. Data collected at our university (Illinois State at Normal) with a random sample of undergraduate students provide support that these gender differences actually exist (Sprecher, 1986). The respondents were asked a series of questions about how they came to meet and begin dating their last relationship partner. Men were much more likely than women to initiate the first date, be responsible for planning the activities of the date, pay for the expenses of the date, and initiate a second date.

So far we have discussed how couples make initial contact and begin their dating relationship. Next we discuss the factors that affect how attracted two people will be to each other once they have a chance to interact.

ᴥ Attraction

People seek out, ask out, continue to date, and desire to have sex with those to whom they are attracted. For more than 25 years, social psychologists and researchers in related disciplines (e.g., sociology, communication) have been studying the attraction process and identifying the factors that influence initial attraction and mate selection. Only a brief review is possible in this chapter, but the reader is encouraged to explore more extensive reviews of the theory and research in this area, including Berscheid (1985), Brehm (1992), Hendrick and Hendrick (1992), and Surra (1990).

An Overview of Methods
Used to Study Attraction

Researchers have used several methods to identify the factors important in the initial attraction process. A brief overview will give an idea of the ingenuity of researchers in this field in answering research questions (e.g., "What factors lead to attraction?").

1. *Experiments.* Subjects are asked to report how attracted they are to an opposite-sex person (most often, a bogus other—that is, someone who really does not exist), based on limited information presented about him or her, such as his or her physical appearance (e.g., Snyder, Berscheid, & Glick, 1985; Sprecher, 1989a).

2. *Mate selection questionnaires.* Subjects are given a list of possible traits (e.g., kind, intelligent, good-looking) in a questionnaire format and are asked to indicate how much they desire each in a potential partner (e.g., Buss & Barnes, 1986; Howard, Blumstein, & Schwartz, 1987).

3. *Get-acquainted date studies.* Men and women who have not met previously are paired randomly and go on a brief date, after which each partner separately completes a questionnaire that asks how much attraction he or she feels toward the other (e.g., Byrne, Ervin, & Lamberth, 1970; Walster [Hatfield], Aronson, Abrahams, & Rottman, 1966).

4. *Content analysis of personal ads.* Researchers sample a number of personal advertisements actually placed in newspapers and magazines in order to identify the kinds of traits people offer and request in a partner (e.g., Harrison & Saeed, 1977; Koestner & Wheeler, 1988).

5. *Choices made in videodating services.* Members of videodating services are asked to explain what attracts them to certain others after they screen initial material (photographs and brief biographies) or the others' videotapes (e.g., Woll, 1986).

6. *Retrospective accounts.* People who recently have experienced attraction or love for another are asked to think back and report on what initially attracted them to the other person (e.g., Aron, Dutton, Aron, & Iverson, 1989).

Predictors of Romantic Attraction

Let us return to Shelley in the scenario presented earlier. What factors predict the likelihood that she will be attracted to the man by the keg, whom we now identify as Mike? We organize our review of the vast literature on determinants of initial attraction around Kelley et al.'s (1983) close relationship model. Kelley and his colleagues identified four types of causal conditions that can affect the interaction patterns between two people (Person and Other) in a relationship: Person factors, Other factors, Person × Other factors, and Environmental factors.

Person Factors

Shelley may have certain characteristics that are likely to affect how much she desires to begin a new romantic relationship and how much attraction she feels toward Mike. One such characteristic is Shelley's availability. If Shelley is not currently romantically involved and desires to begin a new relationship, she is likely to feel attraction toward Mike (Berscheid, Graziano, Monson, & Dermer, 1976). Conversely, if she already is dating someone, she is unlikely to feel as much attraction toward Mike and even may devalue him in order not to be tempted to consider an alternative partner (e.g., Johnson & Rusbult, 1989; Simpson, Gangestad, & Lerma, 1990).

Shelley's personality characteristics and psychological states also can affect the attraction process. The following factors are associated with a greater likelihood that she might become attracted to Mike: experiencing emotional loneliness or isolation, which has been defined as the absence of an intense relationship (Weiss, 1973); a high desire for intimacy or affiliation (Weiss, 1969); and temporarily lowered self-esteem (Walster [Hatfield], 1965). Furthermore, Shelley's social skills (e.g., expressivity) will affect how likely it is that she has a rewarding first interaction with Mike (Riggio, 1986; Riggio & Zimmerman, 1991).

Other Factors

We also can consider what it is about Mike that attracts Shelley (and other women) to him. The "other" factor that has been examined most frequently is physical attractiveness (recall that Shelley noticed that Mike "had the body of a runner"). Research shows that people are attracted to those who are physically attractive (for a review of this extensive literature, see Hatfield & Sprecher, 1986b). This relationship has been demonstrated in get-acquainted date studies (e.g., Walster [Hatfield] et al., 1966) and bogus stranger experimental designs (e.g., Sprecher, 1989a). Furthermore, physical attractiveness is one of the most important factors that members of videodating services consider in their decisions about which members they want to meet (Woll, 1986). Physical attractiveness is also often mentioned in personal ads (e.g., Harrison & Saeed, 1977).

Although physical attractiveness seems to have a strong influence on initial attraction, people claim that it is not that important to them in their decisions about whom they want to date or marry; that is, in the mate selection studies (in which subjects respond to a list of characteristics), subjects say that many other characteristics (e.g., expressiveness, dependability) are much more important to them than physical attractiveness (e.g., Buss, 1989c; Buss & Barnes, 1986; Howard et al., 1987). Furthermore, women are less likely than men to say that they value physical attractiveness in a partner (e.g., Feingold, 1990). On the other hand, women value to a greater degree than men the other's social standing or earning capacity (e.g., Buss, 1989c; Buss & Barnes, 1986; Koestner & Wheeler, 1988).

Two theoretical perspectives have been offered to explain these gender differences (e.g., Buss & Barnes, 1986). One explanation is based on *social factors*. According to this perspective, men and women learn to value different traits in a partner because of their different positions and differential access to power in the larger social structure. For example, because women traditionally have been limited in the degree to which they have access to economic resources, they have learned to value earning capacity in a partner. The other explanation is based on principles of *sociobiology*. According to this perspective, males will be attracted to a physically attractive woman because her appearance is a cue to her health and reproductive capacity. Conversely, females will seek out a man who is a good provider because this will assure them that their offspring will have material advantages.

Although our scenario was about Shelley and Mike, it also could have been about Shelley and Shirley, or Mike and Matthew. Contrary to the stereotype that homosexuals, particularly gay men, give unusually high importance to physical attractiveness (Laner, 1977), heterosexuals and homosexuals have been found to rank traits desired in a partner in nearly the same way (e.g., Engel & Saracino, 1986; Howard et al., 1987; Laner, 1977). From a large national sample of homosexual couples and heterosexual married and cohabiting couples, Howard et al. (1987) using the data collected from Blumstein & Schwartz, 1983 found that homosexuals preferred to a greater degree than heterosexuals a partner who is expressive and athletic. These differences, however, were not large, and no difference was found between homosexuals and heterosexuals in preferences for physical attractiveness.

Person and Other Factors in Combination: Similarity and Matching

In understanding the attraction Shelley experiences for Mike, we also must consider Shelley's and Mike's characteristics in combination. Shelley may be attracted to Mike in particular (rather than to Tom, Dick, or Harry, who are also at the party) because she perceives that his characteristics are similar to and/or match hers.

Similarity on demographic characteristics (e.g., age, race), attitudes and values, physical appearance, and other characteristics leads to attraction. Extensive research conducted during the past several decades has provided support for the proverb "Birds of a feather flock together" (e.g., Byrne, 1971; Newcomb, 1961). Similarity may be attractive for a number of reasons, including that similar others are confirming and we expect to be liked and not rejected by similar others. According to one recent perspective (Rosenbaum, 1986), however, it is not similarity that leads to attraction, but rather that dissimilarity can lead to repulsion.

Similarity sometimes has been called the *matching phenomenon*, although matching does not require similarity. Some couples are not similar but still are matched on degree (but not kind) of socially desirable characteristics. This fit has been called *cross-character matching or assortment* (Buss & Barnes, 1986), and the most common form is gender-linked: Traditionally women have traded their looks and/or youth for men's greater social status and earning potential (e.g., Elder, 1969; Udry & Eckland, 1982). As a recent real-world example of the importance of similarity or matching, consider what Ted Turner's daughter said about her father's marriage to Jane Fonda: "They're just so alike. Both overachievers, both brilliant. Neither one of them outshines the other" (*People*, p. 36).

Environmental Factors

Relationships do not begin in a vacuum. Environmental factors may affect the degree of attraction Shelley experiences for Mike. Both the social environment and the physical environment can have an impact on the initiation of the relationship.

Social environment. When Shelley rejoins the girlfriends who accompanied her to the party, they are likely to offer their opinions of Mike. They might say, "Don't you dare flirt with him. He's not right for you" or, "Wow! You'd better snatch him up before one of us does." Her friends' comments, as well as her own notion of how well Mike fits into her *field of eligibles* (Kerckhoff, 1974), as defined by her family, peers, and society, are likely to influence the degree of initial attraction she experiences for Mike. Most research suggests that the more support Shelley receives from her friends and family to date Mike, the more attraction and commitment she will feel for him (e.g., Eggert & Parks, 1987; Felmlee, Sprecher, & Bassin, 1990; Lewis, 1973; Parks & Adelman, 1983). One study, however, found some support for what has been called the *Romeo and Juliet effect*, the notion that "parental interference in a love relationship intensifies the feelings of romantic love between members of the couple" (Driscoll, Davis, & Lipetz, 1972, p. 1). Thus, under some conditions, parents' opposition to the relationship may increase attraction.

Physical environment. Aspects of the physical environment also can affect initial attraction. For example, picture the following two situations:

> *Situation 1:* The party is packed, and it is difficult to move around. People push and shove to get to the beer keg. It is also a steamy summer night, and the apartment does not have air conditioning. Because the apartment is small, all furniture was moved out to make room for the party guests. As Shelly talks to Mike, she is thinking about how tired she is of standing and how hot and sweaty she feels.

> *Situation 2:* A good crowd was at the party, but the apartment was spacious and could accommodate everyone comfortably. It was a hot summer night, but the air conditioning kept the room at a comfortable 72 degrees. Soft lounge chairs and sofas were scattered through the apartment. As Shelley and Mike were talking, they snuggled down into one of the comfortable sofas.

Research suggests that Shelley will experience more attraction to Mike in Situation 2. Heat, crowding, and other unpleasant environmental conditions reduce the attraction experienced for others in the setting (e.g., Baron, 1987; Griffitt, 1970; Griffitt & Veitch, 1971). Even the type of music playing can have an effect on attraction. Females have been found to judge males as more physically attractive while they are listening to rock music than while they are listening to avant-garde music (May & Hamilton, 1980). Findings showing that attraction for someone can be influenced by the physical environment have been interpreted within a reinforcement-affect model of interpersonal attraction (Byrne & Clore, 1970), which states that a person's attraction (or repulsion) for another is affected not only by his or her direct behaviors but also by the rewards and negative experiences that are associated with him or her; that is, we may come to like another because of his or her positive associations, and to dislike another because of his or her negative associations, such as crowds, noise, and heat.

So far, we have discussed predictors of initial romantic attraction. Next we discuss research on predictors of sexual attraction more specifically.

Predictors of Sexual Attraction

Although romantic attraction may always include some degree of sexual attraction, the latter may be experienced without romance. Do the same factors that predict romantic attraction also predict sexual attraction? In a few studies, predictors of sexual attraction have been compared to predictors of other types of attraction.

Nevid (1984) had subjects rate the desirability of several physical features (e.g., overall attractiveness, weight), demographic characteristics (e.g., age, race), and personal qualities (e.g., sensitivity, honesty, warmth) for two types of relationships: one described as a "sexual relationship" and the other described as a "meaningful or long-term relationship." Both men and women evaluated personal characteristics as more important than physical characteristics in a long-term, meaningful relationship, but physical features were given more importance in a sexual relationship than in a long-term relationship, particularly by men. Kenrick and Trost (1989) described data (based on Kenrick, Sadalla, Groth, & Trost [1990] and Kenrick, Trost, Groth, & Sadalla [1988]) on men's and women's minimum standards for a partner's intelligence in four levels of relationship involvement: single date, sexual relations, steady dating, and marriage. Females were found to increase their standards for intelligence in a partner with each increase in the level of relationship involvement. Their standards were lowest for a single date and highest for marriage. Men, however, expressed their lowest minimum standards for a sexual relationship. They were less selective for a sexual relationship than they were even for a single date. These results are presented in Figure 2.1.

In another study, Townsend and Levy (1990) had subjects judge their willingness to begin six types of relationships that varied in level of sexual involvement and marriage potential for each of three different target persons who varied in level of physical attractiveness and socioeconomic status (earning potential). For all types of relationships, a potential partner's socioeconomic status was a more important predictor of willingness to enter the relationship for women than for men. Physical attractiveness affected willingness to enter the six types of relationships for both men and women, but particularly when the relationship was described as involving sex.

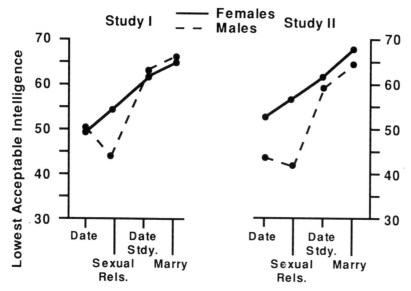

Figure 2.1. Men's and Women's Minimum Standards in a Partner for Intelligence at Four Different Levels of Relationship Involvement (Data presented in Kendrick & Trost, 1989, based on two studies)

Other's Sexual Experience (or Inexperience)
as a Predictor of Attraction

Many years ago, most young women probably got the message from parents and from society that men prefer to marry a virgin over a woman "with experience." Today's young women may no longer be getting these parental messages. Prather (1990) asked approximately 100 college students enrolled in Sociology of Family classes to describe the messages that parents and others gave them concerning the type of person they should marry. The researchers reported: "Surprisingly, there were few comments concerning sexual experience or virginity. Only one student reported his family's insistence that he find a virgin" (p. 90). Students recalled that their parents' messages were focused on the potential mate's religious background, race, and social class or earning capacity.

Do young adults themselves care about the level of sexual experience in a potential romantic partner? We consider two lines of research that have addressed this question.

The Mate Selection Surveys:
Is Chastity Important?

Back in the 1930s, Hill (1945) constructed a list of personal characteristics that were likely to be considered as desirable in a potential
marriage partner. Chastity (no previous experience in sexual intercourse) was included in this list, along with dependable character,
emotional stability, pleasing disposition, good health, good looks,
favorable social status, and several other personal characteristics. The
list was distributed to college students, who were asked to indicate
which characteristics were "indispensable," which were "important
but not indispensable," and which were "desirable but not very
important." Students in the 1930s thought that chastity was a relatively important characteristic for their mate to have. For example,
the average rating that both men and women gave to chastity was
between "important" and "indispensable." Of the 18 factors listed,
chastity was rated 10th in importance and was found to be more
important than such traits as intelligence, sociability, and good looks.
No sexual double standard was found; that is, men and women
valued chastity in a partner to about the same degree.

This same list of personal characteristics was distributed to sub-
sequent generations of college students (e.g., Henze & Hudson, 1969;
Hoyt & Hudson, 1981; McGinnis, 1959). Hoyt and Hudson (1981)
compared their data, collected in 1977, with the original Hill (1945)
data and with the data collected in the intervening years. They found
that chastity declined in importance over the years to a greater
degree than any other characteristic included in the original list. For
example, in 1977, chastity was rated 17th in importance by women
and 18th by men (as compared with 10th in the 1930s).

A similar list of mate selection values was used in a recent cross-
cultural study. In data collected from more than 10,000 men and
women from 33 countries, Buss (1989c) found cross-cultural variation
in how much chastity was desired in a mate. Samples from China,
India, Indonesia, Iran, Taiwan, and Israel were particularly likely to
value chastity in a partner (these samples tended to say that it was
"indispensable"). In contrast, samples from Sweden, Norway, Fin-
land, the Netherlands, West Germany, and France rated chastity as
irrelevant or unimportant. The subjects from North America also rated

chastity as relatively unimportant, although they did not rate it as unimportant as did the samples from the Scandinavian countries.

In his cross-cultural research, Buss (1989c) predicted that men would value chastity in a partner to a greater degree than would women. He based this prediction on a *sociobiological perspective*. According to this approach, males are concerned about mating with someone whose offspring are certain to be the male's own. Knowledge that a potential partner is chaste (at least prior to the current relationship) helps assure a man of his future biological parenthood and also suggests to him that the woman is likely to be sexually faithful. Some support was found for his prediction. In 62% of the samples, men valued chastity to a greater degree than did women. In the remaining 38% of the samples, however, no gender difference was found. (The United States was one of the countries in which a small gender difference was found.)

Experimental Designs:
What About a Little Sexual Experience?

Mate selection research suggests that chastity is relatively unimportant as a mate selection value among today's young adults in the United States. Has the pendulum swung in the other direction? Are people with extensive sexual experience preferred over those who have none or only a little? This question has been examined with the bogus stranger experimental design. In this design, subjects are presented with information about the sexual past of a (hypothetical) opposite-sex person and then are asked to indicate how much they like this other person or would like to date or marry him or her.

In an early study of this type, Istvan and Griffitt (1980) had male and female college students rate the dating and marriage desirability of a hypothetical opposite-sex individual, based on his or her ostensible responses to Bentler's (1968a, 1968b) Heterosexual Behavior Inventory. The experimenter actually completed the inventory and presented the hypothetical individual as either low, moderate, or high in past sexual experience. The subjects also completed the Bentler inventory for their own past sexual behavior. The researchers found that inexperienced male subjects and both inexperienced and moderately experienced female subjects rated a highly experienced opposite-sex individual as less desirable for both dating and marriage than a moderately experienced or inexperienced individual. The ratings given by the more sexually experienced male and female subjects were not affected by the target's ostensible level of sexual experience. The authors concluded that their findings "indicate that knowledge of the sexual experiences of a member of the opposite sex can be a powerful determinant of judgements of the suitability of the person as both a date and spouse" (Istvan & Griffitt, 1980, p. 383).

Jacoby and Williams (1985) replicated and extended the Istvan and Griffitt study. They found that subjects, regardless of their own past sexual experience, generally preferred as a dating and marriage partner an opposite-sex person who had moderate levels of lifetime sexual experience (some petting experience) more than someone who had either extensive experience (sexual intercourse) or no sexual experience. A person presented as having a large number of previous sexual partners and/or permissive sexual attitudes also was considered to be less desirable as a partner. In a second study by the same authors, the previous results were replicated, and it also was found that a person who was presented as having prior homosexual experience was given low dating and marriage desirability ratings (Williams & Jacoby, 1989).

A double standard in marriage preferences assumes that men desire to marry a virgin, whereas women desire to marry a sexually experienced man (e.g., Istvan & Griffitt, 1980). The bogus stranger experimental studies have found very little evidence for this traditional double standard. Istvan and Griffitt (1980) did find that inexperienced men rated a highly experienced woman as less desirable as a marriage partner than a moderately experienced or inexperienced woman, but the sexually experienced men in the study were relatively unaffected by the target woman's level of sexual experience. Furthermore, women did not express a greater desire for sexually experienced men over sexually inexperienced men. In fact, just the opposite was found for the inexperienced and moderately experienced women. They preferred a man with less sexual experience! Jacoby and Williams (1985) and Williams and Jacoby (1989) also found no evidence for the traditional double standard in marriage choices.

A double standard has been found in dating choices, but it is a reverse double standard. Istvan and Griffitt (1980) predicted that women's "value as *dating partners* is enhanced by increasing perceived sexual experience due to the expectations of men regarding their availability for sexual relationships" (p. 378). They suggested, in contrast, that men with sexual experience may be less desirable dating partners because women may worry that such men may be too sexually demanding. In their study, women were found to prefer less sexually experienced men as dating partners, but the results were less clear for the male subjects and generally did not support the prediction. In a study by Garcia (1983), gender-typed (feminine) females were particularly rejecting of a sexually experienced male as a dating partner. Furthermore, Williams and Jacoby (1989) found that a highly experienced man was more rejected than a highly experienced woman for dating.

In the above studies, all subjects were asked to judge a person of the opposite sex. In an experiment conducted with a colleague, we (Sprecher et al., 1991) asked male subjects and female subjects to judge the dating, friendship, and marriage desirability of either a male or a female target (randomly assigned to subjects) after receiving information about his or her sexual behavior in a current relationship. We found that a male was perceived as most desirable as a date when he engaged in moderate sexual activity, whereas a female was perceived as most desirable as a date when she engaged in a high level of sexual activity (see Figure 2.2). These results were found regardless of the gender of the subject. No evidence was found for a double standard in marriage and friendship preferences, however. Both men and women in the study rated the marriage and friendship desirability of someone who had sexual intercourse in a current relationship as less desirable than someone who had not, regardless of the other's sex.

The primary focus of the experimental studies reviewed above was on how the target's previous sexual behavior influences attraction for him or her. Oliver and Sedikides (1992) conducted two experiments to examine the influence of a target's *sexual attitudes* on a person's attraction for him or her. In Experiment 1, men and women were asked to complete the Hendrick and Hendrick (1987c) Sexual Permissiveness Scale (described in the previous chapter) as they

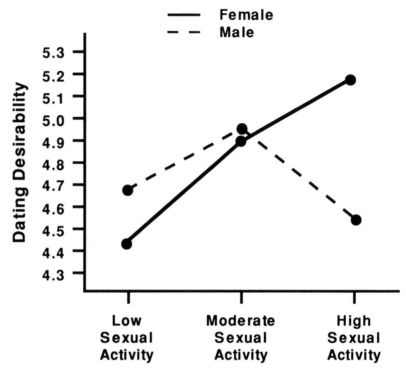

Figure 2.2. How a Person's Desirability as a Date Depends on His or Her Level of Sexual Activity in a Current Relationship (Data from Sprecher, McKinney, & Orbuch, 1991)

would like either a blind date or a spouse (this was assigned randomly) to respond to the items. Although both men and women overall preferred a low level of sexual permissiveness in a partner, men who were assigned to the blind date condition preferred higher levels of sexual permissiveness than did men assigned to the marital partner condition. Women, however, preferred equally low levels of permissiveness for both a blind date or for a spouse.

In their second experiment, Oliver and Sedikides (1992) had male subjects and female subjects rate the desirability of an opposite-sex target based on how the target had ostensibly completed the Hendrick and Hendrick (1987c) Sexual Permissiveness Scale. Subjects were assigned randomly to evaluate either a high permissive target or a low permissive target. Women judged the permissive target less favorably than the nonpermissive target on both dating and marriage desirability. Although men also attributed greater marriage desirability to the nonpermissive target than to the permissive target, they rated the permissive target higher on dating desirability.

In sum, the results from mate selection research show that chastity is no longer judged to be a necessary characteristic in a partner, at least among young adults in many Western countries. The results of bogus stranger experimental studies suggest that a moderate level of sexual experience in a potential partner is more desirable than either extensive sexual experience or no experience. These experimental studies also suggest that men have standards for a date different from those they have for a marriage partner. Men want their dating partner to have sexual experience and, in fact, want more sexual experience in a dating partner than do women.

❧ Summary

In this chapter we reviewed briefly the research on how romantic relationships begin and the factors affecting the attraction process. We delineated three stages of the beginning of the relationship: first seeing, first meeting, and first date.

Men are more direct in their initiation strategies, whereas women tend to be more subtle. Several types of factors affect whether one person (P) becomes attracted to the other (O), including P's characteristics, O's characteristics, P's and O's characteristics in combination (e.g., similarity), and environmental factors. Research that has compared predictors of romantic attraction to predictors of sexual attraction more specifically has found that physical appearance, an important predictor of romantic or general attraction, may be even more important for sexual attraction.

In the last section, we focused on how sexuality may affect the attraction process. More specifically, we examined the degree to which a sexually experienced versus a sexually inexperienced partner is desired. Although virginity or chastity no longer is considered to be indispensable in a partner in Western societies, extensive sexual experience and liberal sexual attitudes are not desirable either. It seems that moderation in sexual experience is most attractive.

This chapter focused on how the relationship begins. In the next chapter we discuss how the sexual aspect of the relationship begins.

3

Beginning Sex in the Close Relationship

In this chapter we discuss how the sexual aspect of the close relationship begins. Questions addressed in this chapter include, How important is the first sexual intercourse experience to the couple? What are the possible sexual pathways on which couples travel? What factors affect the relationship partners' decisions to become sexually involved? How do partners actually initiate sex, and what happens when one partner is ready for sex and the other is not? We also consider whether couples today discuss AIDS and safe sex practices before they become sexually involved.

❧ The First Time

The "first time" for heterosexual couples usually is thought of as the first time they have sexual intercourse. Some heterosexual couples and all homosexual couples, however, give special significance to the first time for other types of intimate sexual behaviors, such as oral-genital sex. Although the first intercourse experience during adolescence or young adulthood (the transition from virgin to non-virgin status) has been the focus of much research (topics examined include age at which it occurs, degree of affection experienced for the partner, reactions to the event, and whether it is discussed with others), very little research has examined the first time for particular couples and how this event is experienced in the relationship. Here we review the limited research on the first time for the couple.

The Sexual Script for the First Time

Imagine that Shelley and Mike, who met at a party in the previous chapter, began a dating relationship and are now at a stage in their relationship when they are about to have sexual intercourse for the first time. A common myth is that sex is a spontaneous act. According to sociologists (e.g., DeLamater, 1989; Gagnon, 1990; Gagnon & Simon, 1973; Reiss, 1989), however, sexual partners follow a *sexual script*, which they have learned from society. A couple's first sexual intercourse experience and later sexual interactions are influenced by the following aspects of the sexual script:

Who: They have chosen a person of about the same age and of the opposite sex (or of the same sex for those who are homosexual). The person is also likely to be from their "field of eligibles"—for example, someone with a similar background (Kerckhoff, 1974).

Where: The couple is likely to have sex in a private location. For example, couples often have sex in a bedroom.

When: They wait until they have been dating for a while. They also have sex at the end of an evening date.

Why: They have sex to express love for each other. They also find it pleasurable.

What behaviors and in what sequence: Couples are likely to engage in a particular sequence of sexual behavior. They begin with passionate kissing, move to breast and genital touching, perhaps have oral-genital sex, and then have sexual intercourse (Geer & Broussard, 1990; Jemail & Geer, 1977).

Of course, not all couples adhere exactly to all aspects of society's common sexual script. Couples also may develop their own idiosyncratic, relationship-specific sexual scripts, which tend to continue throughout their relationship.

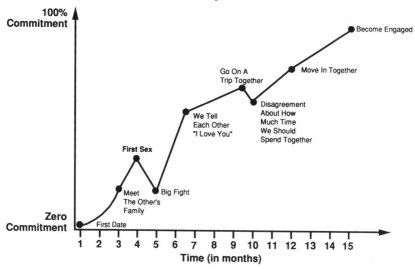

Figure 3.1. Example of Turning Points in a Developing Relationship

The Significance of the First Time

The first sexual encounter often is considered to be a *significant event* or *turning point* in the couple's relationship. Baxter and Bullis (1986) defined a *turning point* as any event associated with change, either positive or negative, in the relationship. They used the Retrospective Interview Technique (RIT) (see Huston, Surra, Fitzgerald, & Cate, 1981), which asks relationship partners to identify all of the turning points in the relationship and to plot those points on a graph similar to the one in Figure 3.1. The *x* axis represents time in the relationship, and the *y* axis represents an index of commitment, such as an estimate of the likelihood of marriage or the degree of commitment. Figure 3.1 depicts a typical individual in a college relationship and indicates that the first sexual experience has a positive effect (after a brief downturn) and increases the person's commitment. Baxter and Bullis (1986) found that events associated with "passion," such as first sex, were among the events having the greatest positive effect on commitment. The graph in Figure 3.1 is for one member of the couple. His or her partner may have a different perception of the occurrence, timing, and effects of the turning points in their relationship.

Significant events, such as first sex, usually are remembered with vivid detail ("flashbulb memory") months and years later. Harvey, Flanary, and Morgan (1986) investigated the memories of a sample of middle-aged adults for the most emotionally significant relationship they had experienced. They reported, "Across subjects, the theme of first sexual encounter turned out to be a predominantly salient memory for both sexes (reported in over 50 percent of all subjects)" (pp. 367-368).

Pathways to the First Time

In the not so distant past, many couples waited until they were married before having sexual intercourse. For example, Kinsey (Kinsey, Pomeroy, Martin, & Gephard, 1953) found that among the women in his study who were born before 1900, 73% did not have sex until they married. Today, some couples, like their great-grandparents (or at least their great-grandmothers) wait for marriage, but most couples have sex at some point on the *dating continuum* (Adams, 1986), which includes the stages of casual dating, serious dating, and engaged.

Researchers have categorized couples according to how soon in the relationship they have sex. Christopher and Cate (1985b) had each partner of 54 dating couples complete Bentler's (1968a, 1968b) Sexual Involvement Scale (which asks about 21 sexual behaviors ranging from *one minute continuous lip kissing* to *mutual oral manipulation of genitals to mutual orgasm*) for four significant points in their relationship. These four points were first date, casually dating, considering becoming a couple, and perceiving themselves as a couple. With this retrospective information, Christopher and Cate identified the following four sexual pathways:

> *Rapid-involvement couples (7%):* These couples had sex very early in the relationship, often on the first date.
> *Gradual-involvement couples (31%):* These couples reported a gradual increase in sexual behavior over the four stages of dating.
> *Delayed-involvement couples (44%):* These couples tended to delay sexual involvement until they considered themselves to be a "couple."
> *Low-involvement couples (17%):* These couples were still not very sexually intimate at the time they felt like a couple.

Earlier, Peplau et al. (1977) developed a typology of sexual pathways, based on the Boston Dating Couples Study, introduced in Chapter 1. They delineated three groups of couples, based on the timing and occurrence of sex. These couples were "early-sex" couples (41% of their sample), who had sex within the first month of dating; "later-sex" couples (41% of the sample), who did not have sex until they had been dating at least 1 month; and "abstaining" couples (18% of the sample), who had not had sex at the time of the investigation.

❧ The Sexual Decision-Making Process

What factors determine whether a couple has sex early in the relationship or waits until later? Couples must decide when they are ready to have sex, and they are likely to weigh several factors in this decision. Some researchers have studied the sexual decision-making process by asking virgins or abstaining couples why they have not yet had sex. Other researchers have surveyed young adults who have made the decision to engage in premarital sex and have asked why they had sex, particularly their reasons for the first time.

Reasons for Not Having Sex

Two types of virgins have been identified, and they give different reasons for not having premarital sex. D'Augelli and her colleagues (D'Augelli & Cross, 1975; D'Augelli & D'Augelli, 1977) distinguished between adamant virgins and potential nonvirgins. *Adamant virgins* have made the decision not to engage in premarital sex because they strongly believe that intercourse should be saved for marriage; that is, they adhere to the abstinence standard that was discussed in Chapter 1. Adamant virgins are influenced strongly by their families and religion. For example, a view expressed by one adamant virgin is: "Premarital intercourse is simply wrong. It should be saved for marriage—marriage is more than a piece of paper. Sex belongs in marriage, according to society" (D'Augelli & D'Augelli, 1977, p. 58). *Potential nonvirgins* say they have not had sex because they have not been in the right situation or in love enough. They also have a fear of pregnancy. They say, however, that they are open to the possibility of engaging in premarital sex. In an extension of this earlier research,

Herold and Goodwin (1981) found that adamant virgins were most likely to give moral or religious beliefs as the primary reason they remain virgins. Conversely, potential nonvirgins rated having not met the right person as the major reason for their virginity status.

Whereas the above research focused on why individuals remain virgins, other research has examined why partners decide not to have sex in a particular dating relationship (regardless of whether they had sex in previous relationships). The woman usually controls the level of sexual activity in heterosexual relationships; that is, if a couple has been together for several months but has not had sex, it is usually because the female partner is not ready yet. In their study of dating couples, Peplau et al. (1977) asked the men and women in the 42 abstaining couples (18% of the sample) to rate the importance of four reasons for not having engaged in sex. "Partner does not wish to have sexual intercourse at the present time" was judged to be an important reason by 64% of the men but by only 11% of the women. Women were more likely than men to rate "It is against my moral or religious convictions" as an important reason (31% for women, 11% for men). Almost half of both men and women rated fear of pregnancy as a major reason, and 22% of the women but only 14% of the men said that it was too early in the relationship.

Today, there is a new reason to avoid premarital sex. Young people receive the message from parents, public health officials, Magic Johnson, and even billboards ("Virgin. Teach your kids it's not a dirty word.") that sex can be dangerous because of AIDS. Some evidence exists that AIDS may be a new reason to abstain from sex. Leigh (1989) asked men and women from the San Francisco area (76% heterosexuals, 24% homosexuals or bisexuals) to rate the importance of various reasons for not having sex. Fear of AIDS was rated by the participants as the most important reason. Of the four different groups surveyed (heterosexuals and homosexuals of both genders), homosexual men rated it highest in importance, and homosexual women rated it lowest in importance.

Motives for Being Sexually Active

Sex for the first time in a particular relationship, though usually a passionate act, typically occurs after some planning and thought.

Both partners in the couple have to decide whether they want to make their relationship a sexual one and how soon to do so. Many couples discuss the decision to have sex before it occurs (Randolph & Winstead, 1988). They may consider several factors in their decision to have sex for the first time.

Christopher and Cate (1984, 1985a) developed a scale, called the Inventory of Sexual Decision-Making Factors, to measure factors that might be considered in the decision to have sex for the first time in a relationship. Students who had previously had sexual intercourse were asked to indicate how important each of 43 items was in their decision to have premarital intercourse for the first time with their most recent sexual partner (data reported in Christopher & Cate, 1984). Students who had not previously had sex were asked to indicate how important each factor would be in their decision to have sexual intercourse with their ideal partner for the first time (data reported in Christopher & Cate, 1985a).

In an analysis of the data from the nonvirgins, Christopher and Cate (1984) found four general reasons underlying the decision to have sex for the first time. These were as follows:

1. *Positive Affection/Communication*
   Example items: "Love for partner," "Number of dates with partner prior to intercourse," "Possibility of eventual marriage."
2. *Arousal/Receptivity*
   Example items: "Participant's physical arousal immediately prior to intercourse," "Partner's physical arousal immediately prior to intercourse," and "Receptivity of participant to partner's sexual advances."
3. *Obligation and Pressure*
   Example items: "Participant's feeling of obligation to have intercourse with partner," "Partner's pressure on participant to have intercourse," "Number of participant's friends engaging in intercourse."
4. *Circumstantial*
   Example items: "Participant's preplanning to increase chance of intercourse," "Amount of alcohol/drugs consumed by partner," "Date was a special event."

Christopher and Cate (1984) compared men and women on their scores on the above four factors. Two gender differences emerged in the importance attached to these reasons for engaging in sex for the first time within a particular relationship. Positive Affection/ Communication items were rated as more important by women than by men, whereas Obligation/Pressure items were rated as more important by men than by women. The researchers also compared groups, who differed on level of prior sexual experience, on the importance attached to the above factors. Positive Affection/Communication was rated as more salient in the sexual decision-making process of the sexually inexperienced subjects than of the sexually experienced subjects, whereas Arousal/Receptivity was judged to be more important by the highly experienced subjects. Similar findings emerged in the data from the students who had not had sexual intercourse and who rated each item according to what they expected would happen once they did become sexually active (see Christopher & Cate, 1985a). Women were more likely than men to rate relationship issues (e.g., love for partner) as a salient issue in their sexual decision-making process for a future first sexual intercourse experience. The virgins in the Christopher and Cate (1985a) study also were asked what level of commitment they anticipated to have with their partner before having sexual intercourse for the first time. The options listed were as follows: casually dating, seriously dating, engaged, and married. Subjects who expected to have sexual intercourse with a partner for the first time at the casual dating stage rated physical arousal and circumstantial factors as more important and relationship factors as less important than other subjects, particularly as compared to those subjects who anticipated first sexual intercourse at marriage.

One common finding in the research on motives people have for sex is that love is a more important sexual motivation for women than for men, whereas men are more motivated than women to have sex out of lust or physical release. Consider the exchange in Box 3.1, which introduced a chapter in Symons's (1979) book on the evolution of human sexuality (p. 286):

BOX 3.1

Diane Keaton: "Sex without love is an empty experience."

Woody Allen: "Yes, but as empty experiences go, it's one of the best."

As reported above, Christopher and Cate (1984, 1985a) found that women scored higher on the Positive Affection/Communication items. In another study (Carroll et al., 1985) men and women were asked the open-ended question, "What would be your motives for having sexual intercourse?" Typical responses given by females were "To show my love for my partner and to feel loved and needed" and "My motives for sexual intercourse would all be due to the love and commitment I feel for my partner." Males were more likely than females to answer with such responses as "need it" and "to gratify myself." Whitley (1988, as reported in Leigh, 1989) asked men and women, "What was your most important reason for having sexual intercourse on the most recent occasion?" He reported that 51% of men but only 9% of women gave lust/pleasure reasons, whereas 51% of women but only 24% of men gave love/emotion reasons.

In the study of San Francisco adults that was introduced in the previous section, Leigh (1989) also asked her respondents to rate how important several reasons were for *having sex*. The three reasons rated as most important by the respondents were as follows: for pure pleasure, to express emotional closeness, and to please partner. Men were found to give more importance than women to all of the following reasons: pleasure, pleasing one's partner, conquest, and relief of tension. Women gave more importance than men to only one reason: to express emotional closeness. Some differences also were found between the homosexual and heterosexual respondents. "Heterosexuals rated reproduction, emotional closeness, and pleasing one's partner as more important than did homosexuals, and homosexuals rated conquest and relief of tension more highly than did heterosexuals" (p. 203). No differences were found between homosexual men and women.

Another study, however, suggests that these particular gender differences in sexual motivations may be limited to young adults. Sprague and Quadagno (1989) surveyed adults aged 22 to 57 years. Among the younger adults in the sample, women were motivated to engage in sex to express love, whereas men were motivated by physical factors. These gender differences, however, were reversed among the older adults in the sample. These findings support the belief that although a man is at his sexual peak around age 20, a woman's desire is strongest in her mid to late 30s.

Whereas research has shown that young women attach more importance than men to love as a reason to have sex, and young men attach more importance than women to physical reasons, these gender differences are not very large. Men also have sex for love, and women get physical pleasure from sex. It is interesting, though, to speculate on what might have been found had these studies been conducted 150 to 200 years earlier. The gender differences probably would have been even more pronounced, particularly concerning the physical motive for sex. The image we have acquired of the Victorian (19th century) middle-class woman is passionless. During the Victorian era, it was assumed that women did not get pleasure from sex. Degler (1974), a historian, described the story of a 19th century young English woman who asked her mother how she should behave on her wedding night. The mother advised her to "lie still and think of the Empire" (p. 467). Reiss and Lee (1988) reported that an American medical doctor told his medical class in 1883, "I do not believe one bride in a hundred, of delicate, educated, sensitive women, accepts matrimony from any desire for sexual gratification; when she thinks of this at all, it is with shrinking, or even with horror, rather than with desire" (Parven, 1883, p. 607). A study that was uncovered at the Stanford University archives, however, suggests that Victorian women may have been more sexual than this image suggests. The survey was conducted by Dr. Clelia Mosher. Her survey, which may have been the first sex survey, was conducted during the period from 1892 to 1920, with 45 well-educated, middle-class women. A majority of the women felt desire for sex, and many of the women reported usually experiencing an orgasm. An example comment written by a woman: "The desire of both husband and wife for this expression of their union seems to be the first and highest reason for intercourse" (Degler, 1980, p. 264).

Now that we have discussed the *why* of first sexual encounters in close relationships, we will discuss *how* sex gets initiated and *by whom*.

⁊ The Initiation and Negotiation of Sex

Sex, and particularly the first experience of intercourse, does not just happen. The precursors of sex include nonverbal and verbal cues of sexual interest and intent. Furthermore, the pathways to sexual involvement have misperceptions and misunderstandings. These are the issues discussed in this section.

Flirting in Public Places

Social scientists have observed the process by which men and women send each other nonverbal signals that suggest they would like to begin or advance their intimate contact. In one study, Perper and Fox (1980) spent hundreds of hours in singles bars on the East Coast, watching how men and women meet for the first time and, in some cases, leave the bar together. From their observations of the nonverbal behavior in the singles bars, Perper and Fox (1980) concluded that successful flirtation depends on negotiating several escalation points. At each escalation event, the flirtation either escalates upward toward greater intimacy, or the budding romance ends.

The first escalation stage is *approach*. One person approaches the other, and the person approached must respond in some way, such as by moving toward the approaching person or by tilting his or her head. The second stage is *swivel and synchronize*. In this stage the two swivel to face each other and begin to synchronize their movements (he raises his glass, and then she raises hers). The third stage is *touch*. One partner touches the other, and the other must respond positively for the relationship to continue. The researchers found that the women were more likely than the men to touch first.

From in-depth interviews conducted with a smaller sample of men and women, Perper and Fox (1980) also found that the women were more aware than the men of what occurred during flirtation. For example, the women could point to specific behaviors that they had done to attract the attention of a man. Men, on the other hand, were more oblivious to the sequence of behaviors that resulted in the man and woman leaving the bar together.

Another observational study of flirting was conducted by Moore (1985), who recorded nonverbal acts engaged in by women that resulted in a man's attention within 15 seconds after the behavior. In her first study, she identified 52 distinct behaviors that females engaged in that seemed to result in male attention. Some of the more common flirting behaviors were the smile, laugh, room-encompassing glance, short darting glance, head nod, primp, lean, and solitary dance. (You might reread the scenario from Chapter 2 and identify Shelley's flirting behaviors.) In a second study, Moore observed women in four different settings for nonverbal solicitation. The average number of flirting acts per woman during an hour of observation was 70.6 in a singles bar, 18.6 in a snack bar, 9.6 in a library, and 4.7 in a woman's meeting. Moore also found that women who engaged in more nonverbal solicitation behaviors were more likely to be approached by men.

Misperception of Sexual Intent

Although both men and women at singles bars, parties, and other social settings may flirt with others to show romantic or sexual interest, sometimes people are not flirting but only are being friendly. Their friendly behavior may be misinterpreted as flirting or seductive behavior. It has been stated that "in American society it is difficult to distinguish friendly cues from sexual cues" (Abbey, 1991, p. 96).

Several years ago, Abbey (1982) began an article with an account of an event that had occurred to her. She wrote:

> One evening the author and a few of her female friends shared a table at a crowded campus bar with two male strangers. During one of the band's breaks, they struck up a friendly conversation with their male table companions. It was soon apparent that their friendliness had been misperceived by these men as a sexual invitation, and they finally had to excuse themselves from the table to avoid an awkward scene. What had been intended as platonic friendliness had been perceived as sexual interest. (p. 830)

To examine whether this misinterpretation of female friendly behavior occurs, Abbey (1982) conducted a laboratory experiment in which a male subject and a female subject interacted for 5 minutes while they were observed through a one-way mirror by another male and female. After the conversation, the subjects judged the conversation, as well as each other. The observers also judged the subjects. Abbey was interested particularly in how the interacting subjects were judged on the adjectives *flirtatious, seductive*, and *promiscuous*. Abbey found support for her hypothesis that men interpret women's friendliness as sexual interest. The female subject was seen as more promiscuous and seductive by male subjects and observers than by female subjects and observers. Males also attributed more sexual intent to the male subject than did the females. Another gender difference found was that males were more sexually attracted to the female subject than the females were to the male subject.

The basic finding that men are more likely than women to see the world through "sexual glasses" (e.g., Abbey, 1982) has been replicated in several other studies. Abbey, Cozzarelli, McLaughlin, and Harnish (1987) found that males had higher ratings than females of a woman's sexual interest regardless of what the woman was wearing (revealing or nonrevealing clothing) and regardless of whether she was pictured (in a photograph) as interacting with another female or with a male. Saal, Johnson, and Weber (1989) suggested that men's perceptions (misperceptions) of women's flirtatious behaviors may occur in a variety of organization settings, including business and academic settings. Shotland and Craig (1988) demonstrated that males are capable of differentiating between sexually interested behavior and friendly behavior but that males perceive more situations as sexual than do females. They concluded that men have a lower threshold than women for labeling friendly or interested behavior as having a sexual intent. For other research on gender differences in sexual intent, see Abbey and Melby (1986) and Sigal, Gibbs, Adams, and Derfler (1988).

Whereas most of the above studies were conducted in the laboratory (with photographs, videotapes, or subjects interacting in structured situations), Abbey (1987) conducted survey research with undergraduate students to examine the prevalence of misperceptions of sexual intent in real-world settings (at least the real-world setting of college). The college students completed a questionnaire about their experiences with misperceptions of sexual intent. The key question asked was, "Have you ever been friendly to someone of the opposite sex only to discover that she or he had *misperceived* your friendliness as a sexual come-on; you were just trying to be nice but she or he assumed you were sexually attracted to him or her?" She found that about two-thirds of the students reported that this had happened on at least one occasion. The average number of incidents for those reporting at least one incident was 4.8. More women (72%) than men (60%) reported an episode of misperception of sexual intent. The most common location for a misperception was a party.

Abbey (1987) reported that most of the incidents of misperception were brief and nontraumatic. She described the typical experience for a woman in the following way:

> Within the last six months a casual friend touched or kissed her while they were talking at a party. She told him she was not interested in him in "that way." He kept trying or acted as if nothing had happened. No sex occurred; they eventually went their separate ways but remained friends. (p. 190)

Sexual Initiation Strategies in Private

Although a couple's initial contacts and flirting behaviors often occur in public locations, once the partners are at the point of actually initiating sex, they are typically in a private location. Not surprisingly, observational studies of the initiation strategies used in actual sexual encounters are nonexistent. Thus our knowledge of what moves are made and which gender typically makes them are based on self-report data only.

Self-report data suggest that early in the relationship, men are more likely than women to initiate sex (this does not change much later in the relationship, as we will discuss in Chapter 5). For example, DeLamater and MacCorquodale (1979) interviewed a random sample of students and nonstudents from Madison, Wisconsin, and found that approximately 40% of the respondents said the man usually initiated sexual intercourse, whereas less than 5% of the sample said the female typically initiated sexual activity. (Over half of the respondents reported that both partners initiated sexual intercourse.) Grauerholz and Serpe (1985) reported that men feel more comfortable than women initiating sex, and this was true regardless of the type of relationship (e.g., with someone known well or with a stranger). Furthermore, Gaulier, Travis, and Allgeier (1986, as reported in Allgeier & Royster, 1991) found that men are more likely than women "to describe themselves as attempting to move toward greater sexual intimacy and to arouse the partner" (p. 137).

How do men and women initiate sexual activity? McCormick (1979) asked young men and women to describe how they would attempt to have sex with someone to whom they were attracted. Both men and women preferred to use indirect strategies for initiating sex. *Seduction,* an indirect strategy, was the strategy most preferred by the subjects. This term refers to sexually stimulating the dating partner to get the date to want to have sex. Other indirect strategies the subjects reported that they would be likely to use included *sitting closer* and *holding hands.* Jesser (1978) found that the most common strategies both men and women said they would use to try to persuade a partner to have sex was *touching* (snuggling, kissing, etc.) and *allow hands to wander. Ask directly* was the third most common strategy checked (from a list of 20 possible strategies).

In another study, Perper and Weis (1987) asked female college students in the United States and Canada to write an essay describing how they would seduce a man to whom they were attracted. The major proceptive strategies ("female behavior patterns which initiate or maintain sexual interactions") identified by Perper and Weis were (a) environmental/situational strategies (dressing in a seductive way, offering the man a drink, creating a romantic setting), (b) verbal strategies (engaging in sexy/romantic talk, giving compliments, asking for sex), and (c) nonverbal strategies (eye glances, cuddling close, touching, kissing). Although the women's actual behaviors were not examined, the researchers believed that the detail and length of the essays written suggested that women may be more proceptive in sexual interaction than had been assumed in the past. Consider, for example, the essay written by one woman interviewed by Perper and Weis (1987):

> I attempt to influence the mood of my date by suggesting that we go somewhere quiet, relaxing, and secluded. If my date likes this suggestion, I usually let him suggest the place in order to get a better idea of where his head is. If he asks for suggestions as to where to go, I inevitably suggest MY PLACE!
>
> Once we've gotten settled wherever we decided to go I try slipping in compliments whenever I can. These compliments are usually about my date's physical appearance and how it/they turn me on, e.g., your eyes have such a mysterious gleam, they are really captivating; or, your smile is so warm and comforting it just makes me melt. Then after careful evaluation of my date's reaction to all of this I proceed in one of two ways: (a) If his response is positive then I escalate the level of intimacy through more intense eye contact and more but

subtle body contact. This is almost always sufficient to eventually make my date suggest or attempt sex; (b) If his response is either negative or apparently indifferent I will back off a bit and wait for him to make the next move. If he takes too long to do this to suit me, I'll try putting on romantic or soft music and suggesting we dance or I'll offer a body massage to sort of break the ice. I find hoping and praying useful at this point. (p. 468)

Although the previous studies asked participants to report what they would do in an imaginary situation, Christopher and Frandsen (1990) examined the sexual influence strategies that men and women actually used on their last date. Undergraduate students completed a 48-item Sexual Influence Tactics Scale. For each item, subjects responded on the basis of tactics they used during any sexual encounter that may have occurred during their last date. Factor analysis of the 48 items indicated four general influence strategies, labeled by the investigators as *Antisocial Acts* (e.g., verbally or physically threatened my partner, made my partner feel guilty, pleaded), *Emotional and Physical Closeness* (e.g., told partner how much I loved him or her, acted seductively, did something special for my partner), *Logic and Reason* (e.g., asserted my authority, used logic, insisted on the level of sexual involvement, compromised with my partner), and *Pressure and Manipulation* (e.g., used alcohol and/or drugs to more easily influence my partner, manipulated my partner's mood, I talked fast and told white lies). Men were significantly more likely than women to have used pressure and manipulation, but no gender differences were found in the use of the other influence strategies. Both men and women reported that they were more likely to engage in the behaviors emphasizing emotional and physical closeness than the behaviors included in any of the other three factors. Furthermore, of the four sexual influence strategies, emotional and physical closeness was related most strongly to level of sexual activity, which suggests that "these techniques were successful at increasing sexual involvement" (p. 98).

Resistance Strategies

Dating partners do not always have similar expectations and desires for sexual involvement in the relationship. Traditionally males have preferred to have sex early in the relationship, whereas women have preferred to wait. Many years ago, Ehrmann (1959) stated that women have "negative control" in their relationships through their refusal of sex. Women also have been called the "gatekeepers" to the couple's sexuality (Peplau et al., 1977). When partners have different sexual goals and desires, it is likely that one partner (usually the female, in heterosexual relationships) occasionally will have to engage in rejection strategies in response to the sexual initiation attempts of the partner. Researchers have found that women feel more comfortable than men in saying no to a partner who wants sex (e.g., Grauerholz & Serpe, 1985; Zimmerman, Sprecher, Langer, & Holloway, 1992) and also are perceived to be more likely to say no (e.g., McCormick, 1979).

How do men and women say no or signal that they are not interested? One way a person can avoid unwanted sex is to avoid situations in which sex might occur. For example, some women say they would avoid sex by avoiding a private or intimate situation and by not engaging in proceptive (e.g., flirting) behaviors with a man (Perper & Weis, 1987). One 19-year-old woman from the Perper and Weis (1987) study wrote:

> Try to keep your distance as much as possible. No body contact what-soever. Gear your conversation toward mundane topics, such as the weather, the place you're at, etc. Act really uninterested. The point will come across. No invitations back to your apartment, just a thank you and good-bye. (p. 471)

But what happens when an intimate setting cannot be avoided and a sexual advance is made by one partner and the other does not want sex? Research suggests that direct (verbal) strategies are more common than indirect (nonverbal) strategies when resisting sex (McCormick, 1979). What if *you* are the one making the sexual advances and the other rejects you? What type of rejection strategy would be easier to take? Imagine yourself in the following situation: You are alone with someone you find attractive in a sexual-romantic way. You move very close to him or her, hoping that this move will communicate your sexual desire. Now further imagine that this other person is not interested and resists your sexual initiation attempt. Which of the following strategies would you most prefer that your partner use to turn you down?

"Change channel" strategy (diversion): Your partner pretends not to notice your move and asks you to change the channel on television.

"Not good" strategy: Your partner moves away from you and says, "I'm sorry, this just would not be good for our relationship."

"Not attracted" strategy: Your partner moves away and says, "I'm sorry, I just don't feel sexually attracted to you."

"Not ready" strategy: Your partner moves away and says, "I'm sorry, I just don't think I'm ready for this right now."

Metts, Cupach, and Imahori (1992, p. 8) identified the above four rejection strategies after reviewing earlier literature on sexual initiation and refusal and conducting a pilot test with undergraduate students who were asked how they would resist unwanted sex. They conducted an experiment in which subjects read a scenario similar to the one above and then provided their reactions to the rejection. Different versions of the scenarios were created. The "not ready" and "not good" strategies were perceived by the subjects to be more appropriate than the other two strategies. The "not attracted" strategy was considered to be the most direct but also the most constraining (e.g., unexpected, discouraging, embarrassing). All of the rejection strategies were perceived to be more appropriate and less constraining if the relationship was described as a "friendship" rather than as a dating relationship or as ambiguous ("casual friendship that held the prospect of potentially developing into a dating relationship"). Finally, male and female subjects had different reactions to being rejected. Females believed, to a greater degree than males, that being sexually rejected would be constraining; that is, they thought it would be uncomfortable, unexpected, discouraging, and embarrassing. These authors discussed how sexual rejection can often be problematic because the person who resists the sexual advances must make sure that the other gets the message ("I don't want to have sex"), yet at the same time he or she is likely to try to avoid harming the relationship and the other's self-esteem.

Sexual Miscommunication

It has been suggested that, in their rejection strategies, women are sometimes saying, "Please persist." Female token resistance to sex seems to be a part of the script for the first sexual interaction. Muehlenhard and Hollabaugh (1988) examined whether there is any credence to the common belief that women offer token resistance to sex—that is, they say no even though they mean yes. To examine this notion, the authors asked a group of female undergraduate students how often they had been in the following situation:

> You were with a guy who wanted to engage in sexual intercourse and you wanted to also, but for some reason you indicated that you didn't want to, although you had every intention to and were willing to engage in sexual intercourse. In other words, you indicated "no" and you meant "yes." (p. 874)

The authors found that, of the 610 female participants in their study, 240 (39%) had engaged in token resistance at least once and more than half of these 240 women had done this more than once. (A similar percentage, 37%, was found by Muehlenhard & McCoy, 1991.) In the Muehlenhard and Hollabaugh study, women also were asked to rate in importance 26 possible reasons for saying no when they meant yes. The reasons most frequently cited for engaging in token resistance to sex were practical ones, such as not wanting to appear promiscuous. In research conducted by Sprecher, Hatfield, Potapova, Levitskaya, and Cortese (1992), token resistance to sex was examined in three countries: the United States, Russia, and Japan. In the United States sample, 38% of the women said yes to a question similar to the one presented above (note that this is nearly the same percentage found by Muehlenhard & Hollabaugh, 1988). The percentage of women who had engaged in token resistance to sex was slightly higher for the Russian women (59%) but approximately the same in the Japanese sample (37%) as was found in the United States sample.

In our research, we also examined whether men sometimes say no when they mean yes. Although cultural stereotypes suggest that men are always willing to say yes to sex, we found that a large number of men in all three countries had engaged in token resistance to sex. The percentages for the male respondents in the three countries were 47% for the United States, 48% for Russia, and 21% for Japan.

Saying no but meaning yes is not the only form of sexual miscommunication. Sometimes individuals may do just the opposite: They may say yes but mean no. In other words, they agree to have sex despite the fact that they do not want it. How common is this form of miscommunication? The respondents in our cross-cultural study also were asked:

> Has the following situation ever happened to you? You were with a person who wanted to engage in sexual intercourse and you did *not* want to, but for some reason you indicated that you did want to. In other words, you indicated "yes" and you meant "no." Has this ever happened to you?

Women in the United States had the highest rate of consent to unwanted sex (44%), as measured by the above item. The percentages found for the other groups were United States men, 33%; Russian women, 23%; Russian men, 33%; Japanese women, 15%; and Japanese men, 16%.

⁀ Negotiating Safe Sex Behavior

At the beginning of this chapter we introduced the notion that much of sexual behavior, particularly initial sexual behavior, is scripted; that is, people are like actors following a script provided to them. According to this perspective, very little of their sexual behavior is truly spontaneous. The question we discuss in this last section of this chapter is, To what degree have couples incorporated safe sex behavior into their sexual script? We discuss two ways that couples can be cautious in the early stages of the relationship: (a) talking about their sexual histories and about AIDS, and (b) requesting that condoms be used.

Talking About Sexual Histories and AIDS

In romantic or potentially romantic couples, talk about previous sexual relationships may traditionally have been considered to be a taboo topic, something that was off-limits for discussion (Baxter & Wilmot, 1985). Research has shown, however, that many modern couples do talk about their previous sexual relationships. For example, in the Boston Dating Couples Study, Rubin and his colleagues (e.g., Rubin, Hill, Peplau, & Dunkel-Schetter, 1980) asked the partners in the 231 dating couples how much they disclosed on 18 different topic areas. One of these topics was "The extent of my sexual experience previous to my relationship with my partner." Fifty-seven percent of both men and women said they had engaged in "full" disclosure on this topic, and slightly more than one-third of the men and women said they had disclosed "some." Only about 10% said they had practically no disclosure. At the time Rubin and his associates conducted their study, however, talk about previous sexual relations was an act of self-disclosure and did not have any significance as a safe-sex behavior. Thus, *when* the partners discussed their sexual histories was not an issue; they probably revealed this information after intimacy had developed. Today, however, young adults are receiving the message from health officials and parents that they should ask a potential partner about his or her sexual history *before* having sex.

Recent survey studies conducted with young adults show that only some young heterosexual adults are asking the recommended questions of their partners. For example, Edgar, Freimuth, Hammond, McDonald, and Fink (1992) reported that a majority of a sample of sexually active men and women were not confident that they knew the number of their partner's previous sexual relationships. In a sample of 100 dating couples, Sprecher (1991) found that only about half of the sample responded that they were at least slightly more likely to ask their current partner about his or her previous sexual contacts because of the threat of AIDS.

The results of one study suggest that other strategies for seeking information about a partner's sexual past might be used before direct questioning. In a sample of college students, Gray and Saracino (1991) found that only 27% of the students said they are likely to ask a new sexual partner how many previous sexual partners they have had. A majority of the students (60%) said they are likely to "try to guess" whether a new partner had been exposed to AIDS. Metts and Fitzpatrick (1992) discussed other techniques that might be used to reduce uncertainty about a partner's previous sexual history. In addition to the strategy of interrogation (asking the partner directly), the other strategies that might be used include self-disclosing to get the partner to reciprocate, asking others in the social network about the partner, and observing the partner in certain situations to see how he or she responds.

Although a person may ask a potential partner about his or her sexual history, the person may not get the entire truth. Cochran and Mays (1990) surveyed 655 college students from Southern California and found that among the 196 sexually active men and 226 sexually active women in the study, 20% of the men and 4% of the women would lie about the results of an HIV-antibody test, and 47% of the men and 42% of the women would underestimate the number of previous partners.

Some couples do not talk about sexual histories but may talk about AIDS more generally. For example, Sprecher (1991) found that approximately three-fourths of dating partners in one sample said they had talked to their partner about AIDS. Bowen and Michal-Johnson (1989) found that 56% of a college sample reported that they talked about AIDS in a relationship. Cline, Johnson, and Freeman (1992) (also discussed in Cline, Freeman, & Johnson, 1990) further examined the nature of talk about AIDS in dating relationships and identified four groups:

Safe-sex talkers (21% of the sample): These individuals reported that they talked with their sexual partner about AIDS as it applied to their relationship. For example, they talked about sexual histories, condom use, and AIDS prevention within the context of their relationship.
General AIDS talk (43%): These individuals talked about AIDS topics but not in the context of their own relationship.
Nontalkers (32%): These individuals reported that they had not discussed AIDS with a sexual partner and did not desire to do so.
Want-to-be talkers (5%): These individuals reported that they had not discussed AIDS with their partner but wanted to.

Incorporating Condoms Into the Sexual Script

How do people get the message across to their partner that they want to use condoms? As discussed by Metts and Fitzpatrick (1992), Adelman (1991), and others, expressing to a partner one's desire for the use of condoms may be difficult because it may suggest that one does not trust the partner or may send a message about one's own sexual behavior outside the relationship. Adelman (1991) suggested that play and humor be used in requests for condom use. Research conducted by Edgar and Fitzpatrick (1988) suggests that gay men may be particularly adept at discussing condom use.

One recent study (Metts & Cupach, 1991) examined how women would ask their partner to use condoms. Females read a scenario that went like this:

> Tonight you have a date with a man to whom you are attracted. You have dated before, but have not had sex with him. From things he has said, you gather that before dating you, he dated several women during the past year. He has been showing sexual interest in you and you are aroused by him, but you have avoided having intercourse with him so far. You anticipate that tonight might be the first time you have intercourse with him. You want to practice "safe sex" but suspect that he might not automatically wear a condom. How would you go about getting him to wear a condom? What would you say? What would you do to achieve your objective; that is, what steps would you go through to get him to wear a condom, even though he may resist? (p. 12)

Half of the women received the above version, and half received a similar version except that it said the man had been dating one woman exclusively for a year. (Data also were gathered from males about resistance to condom requests.)

The most common technique that females listed for seeking condom use in their male partner was the direct request ("If you want to have sex with me, you must wear a condom"). This finding may seem incongruent with the more general finding, as discussed earlier in this chapter, that indirectness is common in sexual negotiations (e.g., McCormick, 1979; Perper & Weis, 1987). Commenting on this, Metts and Cupach wrote: "Review of the plans in their entirety reveal that the direct request seldom appears alone, but is typically preceded by at least one other more subtle element (e.g., hinting/joking, ingratiation) and often followed by more remedial elements (e.g., providing and assisting with a condom)" (p. 18). Thus a sequence of verbal and nonverbal behaviors probably is involved in the request for condom use and in its acceptance.

Summary

We discussed in this chapter how two people move from being attracted to each other to being sexual partners. For some couples the path is smooth and relatively free of obstacles, but other couples

may encounter misperceptions, misunderstandings, and miscom-
munications on the way to sexual intimacy. The stages of becoming
sexually involved are based on one or both members planning, scheming, and taking initiative. Although traditionally the male has been
the initiator and planner, the research reviewed in this chapter suggests that women also often play a proceptive role in sexual initiation, although their strategies may be more subtle and less direct
than men's. Furthermore, today, women increasingly are taking the
assertive role in talking about sexual histories and requesting that condoms be used. In the next chapter, we turn to a discussion of sexuality
in the close relationship once the relationship has become a sexual
one.

4

Sexual Behaviors and Satisfaction in Close Relationships

In this chapter we discuss what sexually bonded couples beyond the early stages of their relationship are doing in the sexual part of their relationship and how they feel about what they are (or are not) doing. Most of the research on *sexual behavior* and *sexual satisfaction* has been conducted with married couples, although some research exists on these topics for other types of close couples. Some of the questions addressed are, How often do couples have sex? Does frequency of sex decline with length of relationship, and, if so, why? When couples "make love," what specifically do they do? Are couples in our society generally satisfied with the sex in their relationship? We also discuss the types of individuals and couples most likely to be sexually satisfied in their close relationships, and the relation between engaging in certain sexual behaviors (e.g., oral-genital sex) and sexual satisfaction.

❧ Sexual Behaviors in Close Couples

Most couples spend only a small portion of their shared time engaged in genital contact. As estimated by Ford (1980), "couples spend some 15 minutes per week actually copulating, which would amount to 99.9% of their time doing something else" (p. 49). Yet these 15 minutes, plus the time engaged in foreplay, afterplay, and preparation for sex, are an essential part of most sexually bonded relationships.

Frequency of Sex

People often are interested in how often other couples engage in sex, but it is not something generally discussed, at least not in casual group settings.

The conversation in Box 4.1 illustrates the point:

BOX 4.1

Is This Cocktail Party Conversation Typical?

First Couple: We have sex about two times a week. What about all of you?

Second Couple: Oh, we have sex much more often. Probably about four times a week.

Third Couple: We're happy at once a week.

Fourth Couple: We vary from week to week. Generally twice, but sometimes more, sometimes less.

The above conversation sounds strange, does it not? Such a conversation is unlikely to occur. Yet many couples are curious about how their own frequency of sex compares with that of other couples.

Measurement of Sexual Frequency

Sexual frequency typically is measured in large survey studies by one direct question. For example, in their landmark survey study conducted with a national sample of 969 gay, 788 lesbian, and 4,314 cohabiting and married heterosexual couples, Blumstein and Schwartz (1983) asked the following question: "About how often during the last year have you and your partner had sexual relations?" The options ranged from 1= *daily or almost every day* to 7= *a few times*.

Other researchers have asked about sexual frequency without presenting a set of response options (an open-ended question). For example, the question asked of women in the National Fertility Studies (Trussell & Westoff, 1980; Westoff, 1974) was "In the past four weeks, how many times have you had intercourse?"

Sexual Frequency in Married Couples

Although research on sex has increased dramatically in the past few decades, research on *marital sexuality* has not (e.g., Greenblat, 1983). One issue about marital sex that continues to be investigated, however, is sexual intercourse frequency. This issue has been of interest because of its association with fertility (a topic that interests sociologists in the field of demography) and because it is assumed that sex reflects the quality of the relationship (a topic that interests researchers in the field of marriage and the family).

Rates among newly married (young) couples. Many textbooks and popular books on sexuality and marriage state that young married couples in the United States have sex approximately two to three times per week (e.g., Crooks & Baur, 1990; Hyde, 1990). The data from the landmark sexuality studies conducted by Kinsey and his colleagues (Kinsey, Pomeroy, & Martin, 1948; Kinsey et al., 1953) and Hunt (1974) are most often cited as sources for this statistic. Kinsey and his colleagues interviewed 5,300 men for *Sexual Behavior in the Human Male* (1948) and 5,940 women for *Sexual Behavior in the Human Female* (1953). Although their sample was not random, they attempted to obtain respondents from all walks of life. Twenty years later, Hunt surveyed 2,026 adults randomly chosen from phone directories in 24 cities in the United States. Although Hunt's sample was a probability one, only 20% of those initially contacted agreed to participate. People who agree to participate in a sex study may be different (e.g., more sexually liberal) than people who decline (Morokoff, 1986). Thus one must keep in mind that these samples may not have been representative of the entire U.S. population.

Kinsey et al. (Kinsey, Pomeroy, & Martin, 1948; Kinsey, Pomeroy, Martin, & Gephard, 1953) found that the median frequency of marital sexual intercourse per week was 2.45 for respondents in the 16-25 age group and 1.95 for those in the 26-35 age group. Hunt (1974), more than 20 years later, found a higher level of sexual frequency for each age group than did Kinsey et al. For example, Hunt's youngest age group (18-24) had sex an average of 3.25 times per week. Hunt (1974) wrote: "The data show that there has been an important, even historic, increase in the typical (median) frequency of marital coitus throughout the population" (p. 189). As Hunt explained, various "contemporary forces" liberated marital sexuality over this period. These forces included more general sexual liberation, women's liberation, increases in erotic material (e.g., books, magazines, films), and the availability of more effective contraceptive methods (e.g., the birth control pill was introduced in the early 1960s).

Blumstein and Schwartz (1983) conducted their national (nonprobability) study 10 years after Hunt's study and also found that young married couples had sex relatively frequently. They reported that 45% of their heterosexual couples married for 2 years or less had sex three times per week or more, and another 38% had sex between one and three times per week. For couples married 2 to 10 years, comparable percentages were 27% and 46%.

Data on the frequency of marital sexual intercourse also have been obtained in large-scale studies that focus on childbearing decisions and fertility. These studies, conducted with national probability samples, have found rates slightly lower than those found in the sexuality studies described above. Westoff (1974) analyzed data from a probability sample of women under age 45, interviewed in 1965 for the National Fertility Studies (NFS), and reported that they had sex an average of 6.8 times over a 4-week period (or 1.7 times per week). He further found that a different national sample of women interviewed 5 years later, in 1970, reported that they had sex 8.2 times for a 4-week period (or slightly more than two times per week). This was an increase of 21% in intercourse frequency over 5 years, which provides further evidence that the frequency of marital sex increased in the 1960s. Trussell and Westoff (1980) extended this earlier study by including NFS data for 1975. They found a continued increase of sexual intercourse frequency between 1970 and 1975, although the increase was not as large as during the earlier period. In another study of fertility decision making, Udry (1980) conducted a longitudinal study of women who were all under the age of 30 at the time of the first interview. He reported that the mean frequency of sexual intercourse for a 4-week period was 10.01 in 1974, 8.45 in 1977, and 7.75 in 1978. Thus marital sex for these women declined from around 2.5 times per week to less than twice per week over a 4-year period.

The rates reported in the above studies were based on aggregate data; that is, the data were summarized across respondents. If we examine individual relationships in these samples, however, we find considerable variation in how often married couples had sex. Some married couples were celibate or had sex very infrequently (perhaps only on special occasions), whereas other couples had sex at least daily. This variation occurred even within the first year of marriage. Greenblat (1983) interviewed 80 persons married 5 years or less and reported that "the most striking finding concerning the frequency of intercourse during the first year of marriage is the wide *range* of responses" (p. 291). The monthly intercourse frequency reported by the respondents for the first year ranged from 1 to 45.

The decline of marital sexual intercourse over time.

It's declined. As a friend of mine used to tell me, if you took a piggy bank and put a nickel in for every time you had sex during the first year of your marriage, and then did it for the second year, you would have saved less and less money as the years went on. It's declined considerably, but for reasons of strength, not a lack of interest. We just get tired and preoccupied with things and pressures here and there. We used to make love every night and now we don't. But our relationship hasn't decreased. As I said, the spirit is willing, but the flesh is weak. (a husband interviewed by Blumstein & Schwartz, 1983, p. 200)

A decline in sexual frequency over the course of a relationship and over the course of one's lifetime is probably one of those "sure" things in life—like death and taxes. One sex researcher stated, "It has been observed since ancient times that frequency of intercourse declines with age in human beings" (Udry, 1980, p. 320). It should be noted, however, that although frequency may decline with age, the ability to have and enjoy sexual activities extends across the life span.

In all studies on marital sexual frequency that have included respondents from different age groups and/or respondents married for different lengths of time (*cross-sectional studies*), it has been found that respondents who were younger and/or married for a shorter length of time had sex more frequently than couples who were older and/or were married for a longer period of time (e.g., Blumstein & Schwartz, 1983; Edwards & Booth, 1976; Greeley, 1991; Hunt, 1974; James, 1983; Kinsey et al., 1948; Kinsey et al., 1953; Trussell & Westoff, 1980; Westoff, 1974). For example, Figure 4.1 shows the decline with age found among married respondents (both first marrieds and remarrieds) from the National Survey of Family and Households, which is a large survey study of a national, representative sample of adults, conducted in 1987-1988 (Call, Sprecher, & Schwartz, 1992). *Longitudinal panel studies* (the same people are surveyed more than once over a period of time) also have documented a decline in marital intercourse frequency (e.g., James, 1981; Udry, 1980). Finally, *retrospective studies*, in which couples or individuals are asked how often they have sex now and how often they had sex at earlier times in their relationship, also have documented a decline (e.g., Greenblat, 1983). The decline in sexual frequency may be greatest over the first year of marriage. This phenomenon has been called the "honeymoon effect." For example, James (1981) analyzed diaries kept by newlyweds and found that the median frequency of sex in the first month of marriage was over 17 times, but frequency declined to approximately 8 times per month by the end of the first year. James (1981) hypothesized that the rate declines by approximately one-half across the first year and then takes another 20 years to halve again.

In most of the research examining the decline of marital intercourse frequency over time, the partners' ages and the length of the marriage are treated somewhat interchangeably because age and marriage length are highly correlated in the general population. Therefore it is difficult to know whether a decline over time in sexual intercourse frequency is due to factors associated with the aging process or to factors associated with being in a relationship for a long time (e.g., the novelty wearing off). The following fable suggests that novelty wears off over time in one particular relationship:

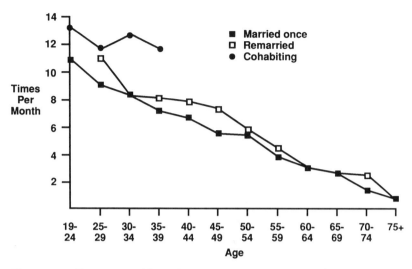

Figure 4.1. Frequency of Sexual Intercourse by Age (Data from Call, Sprecher, & Schwartz, 1992)

One day President and Mrs. Coolidge were visiting a government farm. Soon after their arrival they were taken off on separate tours. When Mrs. Coolidge passed the chicken pens she paused to ask the man in charge if the rooster copulates more than once each day. "Dozens of times," was the reply. "Please tell that to the President," Mrs. Coolidge requested. When the President passed the pens and was told about the rooster, he asked, "Same hen every time?" "Oh no, Mr. President, a different one each time." The President nodded slowly, then said, "Tell that to Mrs. Coolidge." (Bermant, 1976, pp. 76-77)

This fable suggests that if people found a new partner (or several new partners) later in life, they may return to a sexual frequency rate similar to what they experienced at a younger age. On the other hand, we also know that, later in life, ill health and physiological changes can reduce sexual frequency and, in some cases, even can lead to the cessation of sexual activity (Riportella-Muller, 1989). One physiological change that has been blamed for the decline of sexual frequency with age is the decrease in production of androgen, the hormone linked to sexual interest in both males and females (e.g., Udry, Deven, & Coleman, 1982).

In reality, probably both factors—duration of marriage and age of partners—contribute to the decline of sexual intercourse frequency over time. Blumstein and Schwartz (1983) were able to examine the unique effects of both factors in explaining the decline in sexual intercourse frequency. They found that for married couples the impact of age and duration of the relationship were approximately equal. Both negatively affected sexual intercourse frequency and to about the same degree.

Some research has looked at whether the man's age or the woman's age contributes more to the decline in sexual intercourse frequency. Blumstein and Schwartz (1983) reported that the husband's age seemed to have a slightly greater (negative) impact on sexual frequency than the wife's age. Other research has found that the husband's age is more highly associated with the decline (James, 1974; Kinsey et al., 1948; Kinsey et al., 1953), although some research has shown just the opposite (e.g., James, 1983; Udry et al., 1982; Udry & Morris, 1978).

How do couples account for the decline of sexual intercourse over their marriage? Greenblat (1983) examined the accounts that married men and women gave for changes in frequency of sex over the first few years of their marriage. For those married more than 1 year, 69% reported that their current rate was lower than their first-year rate (only 6% reported an increase). She reported that, after the first year, "almost everything—children, jobs, commuting, housework, financial worries—that happens to a couple conspires to reduce the degree of sexual interactions while almost nothing leads to increasing it" (p. 294). The accounts that the respondents provided for the decline in sexual intercourse frequency fell into four major categories: (a) birth-control and pregnancy-related reasons (e.g., "I wasn't interested for a while after the pregnancy, and he got used to it less often"), (b) children (the resulting fatigue and lack of privacy), (c) work (e.g., heavy work schedules, work-related fatigue), and (d) familiarity. Greenblat reported that the most common response in the accounts was familiarity, which sometimes was presented in a negative way (e.g., "We've gotten into a routine with each other, and it's not as exciting anymore"), sometimes in a neutral way, and sometimes in a positive way ("There are other things that satisfy us besides sex: reading to each other, listening to music together . . .").

Rubin (1990) also addressed the question of "What happens to sex in marriage over time?" in her recent interview study conducted with almost 1,000 people from all over the United States. She concluded:

> On the most mundane level, the constant negotiation about everyday tasks leaves people harassed, weary, irritated and feeling more like traffic cops than lovers. Who's going to do the shopping, pay the bills, take care of the laundry, wash the dishes, take out the garbage, clean the bathroom, get the washing machine fixed, decide what to eat for dinner, return the phone calls from friends and parents? When there are children, the demands, complications and exhaustion increase exponentially. And hovering above it all are the financial concerns that beset most families in the nation today. . . .
>
> Even when relative harmony reigns, the almost endless series of tasks, demands, and needs unfilled do nothing to foster the kind of romantic feelings that tend to stimulate sexual desire. "Christ, by the time we get through dealing with all the shit of living, who cares about sex? I sometimes think it's a miracle that we still want to do it at all," said 28-year-old Brian, a Detroit factory worker, married nine years, the father of two small children. (p. 165)

Other factors that affect sexual frequency in marriage. As described above, the number of years married and the ages of partners strongly affect how often married couples have sex. Very few other factors have been found to affect sexual intercourse frequency consistently or strongly. Some social background factors that have been found to modestly decrease sexual intercourse frequency, at least in some studies, include pregnancy, number of children (especially small ones), demanding jobs, being Catholic, living in a rural area, traditional attitudes about sex roles, the female working out of necessity rather than because of career motivations, and not using effective contraceptive methods (e.g., Call et al., 1992; Edwards & Booth, 1976; Trussell & Westoff, 1980; Westoff, 1974).

Do spouses agree about how often they have sex? Spouses do not always agree about how often they have sex. In some research both partners have been asked separately to estimate how frequently they have sex. The correlation between marital partners has been found to range from .60 to .75 (e.g., De Maris & Rao, 1990; Edwards

& Booth, 1976; Udry, 1980). Research suggests that when spouses do not agree about how often they have sex, it is the partner who desires more sex (more often the male) who underestimates the actual frequency, and the partner who desires less sex (more often the female) who overestimates the frequency (Hunt, 1974; Rubin, 1990). For example, in a study by Levinger (1970), wives reported that they had sex almost eight times per month, whereas their husbands reported it as seven times. Research also shows that couples who are less satisfied with their sex life disagree more about the frequency (Rubin, 1990).

Even when two partners can agree about the frequency, they may interpret it differently. Hatfield and Rapson (1993) described a scene from *Annie Hall*. "Woody Allen and Diane Keaton, his lover, are shown on a split screen talking to their respective psychiatrists. 'How often,' the psychiatrists ask, 'do you have sex?' 'Almost never,' complains Woody,—'about twice a week.' 'Oh, all the time,' laments Diane, 'at least twice a week.' "

Sexual Frequency in Cohabiting Couples

The number of unmarried heterosexual couples who live together has increased dramatically in the past few decades. In a number of studies, sexual frequency in cohabiting relationships has been compared with sexual frequency in marital relationships. One problem with making these comparisons, however, is that cohabiting couples eventually either marry or break up, which makes it difficult to find cohabiting couples who have been together for a long period of time. Thus cohabiting couples most often are compared with married couples who are in their first years of marriage.

Blumstein and Schwartz (1983) found that cohabiting couples had sex more frequently than married couples. For example, although 45% of the married couples married 2 years or less had sex three times or more per week, the measure for cohabiting couples was 61% (shown in Figure 4.2). Other studies also have found that cohabitors have sex more frequently than marrieds. Newcomb (1983) reviewed findings from several studies (e.g., Perlman & Abramson, 1982) conducted in the 1970s and early 1980s on cohabiting relationships and reported that cohabitors had a greater frequency of sexual

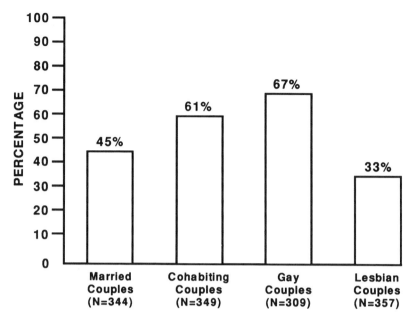

Figure 4.2. Percentage of Couples in Their First Two Years Together who Have Sex Three Times a Week or More (Data from Blumstein & Schwartz, 1983)

intercourse than married couples. In fact, Figure 4.1, based on the data from the National Survey of Family and Households (Call et al., 1992), also shows that cohabiting couples have sex more frequently than married couples. Cohabiting couples also experience a decline in sexual intercourse frequency with increasing age.

Cohabiting couples also may have sex more frequently than dating couples. Results of the Boston Dating Couples Study indicate that, of the 40 couples who were living together, approximately 40% reported having sex six times or more per week. Among the dating couples, however, the measure was 12% (Risman, Hill, Rubin, & Peplau, 1981).

There are at least two explanations for why cohabiting couples may be more sexually active than married couples (and dating couples). First, the individuals who are the "kind of people" who cohabit may be different from people who do not cohabit in ways that would explain the differences in sexual frequency. For example, cohabitors are likely to be sexually liberal and to have liberal sex roles, attitudes that are associated with more frequent sex. Second, a cohabiting relationship may be a "sexier" living arrangement (Blumstein & Schwartz, 1983). Fewer constraints and inhibiting factors in cohabitation, plus the uncertainty of the future of the relationship, may make the relationship more exciting and passionate.

Sexual Frequency in Dating Couples

We have very little data on how often dating couples have sex. Most studies on sexuality in dating relationships have examined the incidence (whether or not the couples engage in sex) but not the frequency. There are some exceptions, however.

Above, we reported that Risman et al. (1981) found that 40% of the cohabiting couples but only 12% of the dating couples from the Boston Dating Couples Study had sex six times or more per week. In the major report on the sexuality of the couples from this study, Peplau et al. (1977) reported that the "early-sex" couples, those who had sex relatively early in the relationship (e.g., after 1 month), had sex at a median frequency of four to five times per week. The "later-sex" couples had sex at a lower frequency, about two to three times per week. In another recent study of sexuality in dating couples, a lower frequency was found. From an analysis of the data from a sample of 94 sexually active couples described in Simpson and Gangestad (1991), Simpson (personal communication, February, 1992) reported that the frequency of sex per month for these dating couples was slightly over seven times per month (or less than twice per week). Dating couples may have sex less frequently than cohabiting couples because they have fewer opportunities and less privacy to do so.

If we consider all types of sexual activity (not just sexual intercourse), however, we may find that dating partners have their hands on each other more than do even cohabiting partners. On the basis of her recent interview study, Rubin (1990) wrote:

> Sexual interest and activity are at their height during dating and courtship, take a drop when people begin to live together, then another

fall after marriage, and show the most precipitous decline after the first child is born. It may be more or less dramatic, more or less troublesome to the particular individuals involved, but the patterning of the response is undeniable. (p. 163)

Sexual Frequency in Homosexual Couples

Figure 4.2 presents data from the Blumstein and Schwartz (1983) study on the percentage of lesbian and gay couples who had sex (genital or oral) very frequently (three times or more per week) during their first years together. As seen in Figure 4.2, the gay couples had sex more frequently than all other couple types, whereas the lesbian couples had the least frequent sex. Lesbian couples, however, engaged in more nongenital physical contact, such as cuddling, touching, and hugging. Blumstein and Schwartz (1983) also reported that by the time they had been together 10 years or more, gay couples had sex less frequently than the married couples. The gays in more long-term relationships were still very interested in sex, but many now were having sexual contacts outside of their primary relationship. Although Blumstein and Schwartz (1983) reported that lesbians had the lowest frequency of sex of all couple types in their study, not all studies have found low sexual frequency among lesbians. For example, Coleman, Hoon, and Hoon (1983) found that lesbian women had sex more frequently than heterosexual women.

As discussed, marital sexual intercourse frequency declines with number of years married. It also declines in homosexual couples over time (Blumstein & Schwartz, 1983; Peplau, Cochran, Rook, & Padesky, 1978). For example, Blumstein and Schwartz (1983) found that the percentage of gay and lesbian couples who have sex three times or more per week after being together 10 years or more is 11% and 1%, respectively.

Other Patterns in Sexual Behavior

Sex researchers have studied not only how often couples have sex but also the positions they use, how long foreplay and sexual intercourse last, and what other sexual behaviors (e.g, oral-genital sex) are practiced. Below we summarize the data on some of these sexual

behaviors. Most of the research examining these specific aspects of
the sexual script has been conducted with married individuals.

Kissing and Other Foreplay Behaviors

Kissing is sensual, and it's an orifice where a connection can be made.
And I also like the taste. I like tongues. There is never a time I don't want
to kiss. (a wife interviewed by Blumstein & Schwartz, 1983, p. 225)

Couples typically begin their lovemaking by spending time kissing and engaging in other foreplay behaviors, such as stimulating
the breasts and genitals. Usually these behaviors are a prelude to
more intimate sexual behaviors, such as oral-genital sex or sexual
intercourse. Sometimes, however, one or both partners have an orgasm through these sexual behaviors, and the couple does not progress to further genital contact.

When Kinsey did his research in the late 1930s and 1940s, couples
in the United States were spending an average of 10 minutes engaged in foreplay behavior before they had sexual intercourse.
Foreplay behavior was more common among the college-educated
respondents than among the noncollege-educated respondents and
was more common among the younger married couples than the
older married couples. In comparing his results with those of
Kinsey, Hunt (1974) reported that every foreplay behavior had
increased in frequency from the 1940s to the 1970s. Furthermore,
Hunt found very few differences between the college-educated
respondents and the noncollege-educated respondents in the sexual
practices engaged in during foreplay.

Homosexual couples, particularly lesbian couples, spend more
time in the foreplay stage of lovemaking than heterosexual couples.
Blumstein and Schwartz (1983) reported that the percentage of
couples who kiss every time they have sex is 95% for lesbian couples,
80% for heterosexual couples, and 71% for gay couples. Other evidence also indicates that lesbian couples engage in more kissing,
body caressing, and breast stimulation than heterosexual couples.
For example, Masters and Johnson (1979) found that lesbian couples
spent more time kissing, holding, caressing, and in breast stimulation than heterosexual couples. Gay couples also were found to

engage in more body contact, including nipple stimulation, than heterosexual couples.

Positions for Intercourse

My ideal position would be in the female above position with a slow but complete penetration in a rather rhythmic rocking motion, with my legs together, and breasts being fondled. But with prolonged "straight" (missionary position) intercourse, my interest lags. (a woman interviewed by Hite, 1976, p. 277)

I am on top maybe ten percent of the time. . . . I like being on the bottom. It feels better . . . We always finish up in the traditional missionary position. Those missionaries knew something. It was less physical work for the woman. I like to avoid all that physical work. (a wife interviewed by Blumstein & Schwartz, 1983, p. 228)

As these two quotes illustrate, people's preferences for sexual positions vary. It has been stated that there are 529 possible positions for sexual intercourse (cited in Gregersen, 1983). Although innumerable variations in positioning for sexual intercourse (which includes different arm and leg positions) are presented in ancient art and modern erotic manuals, there are only a few basic positions. For a heterosexual couple, these include man-above, woman-above, side-by-side, the sitting position, and rear-entry. The most frequently used position in heterosexual couples, in the past and today in our society, is the man-above.

In Kinsey's study, 70% of the participants had used this position almost exclusively. By the time Hunt conducted his study in the early 1970s, American couples were enjoying a wider variety of intercourse positions. For example, Hunt found that 40% had tried the rear-entry intercourse position (as compared with 10% of Kinsey's sample), and 75% occasionally used woman-above (as compared with one-third of Kinsey's sample). Hunt found the "missionary" position, however, still to be the most frequently used position. Blumstein and Schwartz (1983) found that the heterosexual couples in their sample who did not limit themselves to the missionary position were more sexually liberal and more equal in power. Furthermore the female in such couples was more likely to be physically attractive.

Oral-Genital Sex

> His genitals don't attract me in and of itself. It's who's attached to
> genitalia that I care about. Who owns it, who's wearing it . . . I like going
> down on him. It makes him feel good, truly good. I don't find it un-
> pleasant. I don't say I wish I could do it all the time. I don't equate it
> with a sale at Bloomingdale's. That I could do all the time. But it's not
> like going to the dentist either. It's between two extremes. Closer to
> Bloomingdale's than to the dentist." (a wife interviewed by Blumstein
> & Schwartz, 1983, p. 234)

Cunnilingus (oral stimulation of the female's genitals) and fellatio
(oral stimulation of the male's genitals) are two sexual behaviors
that also have increased for heterosexual couples during the past
few decades. Kinsey reported that approximately 40% of college-
educated husbands and 50% of college-educated wives said they
engaged in oral-genital sex in their marriage. Very few of the noncollege-educated respondents, however, had engaged in oral sex.
Hunt (1974) reported, however, that approximately three-fourths of
the married participants in his study had tried both cunnilingus and
fellatio and that few differences were found between college-educated
and noncollege-educated respondents. More recent studies suggest
that a majority of married couples engage in oral-genital sex at least
occasionally (e.g., Gagnon & Simon, 1987; Newcomer & Udry, 1985;
Tavris & Sadd, 1977). In a study of working-class couples, Rubin (1976)
reported that cunnilingus was practiced more frequently than fellatio, in part because the act of fellatio is incongruent with the socialization the women received to be passive in their relationships with
men. Cunnilingus has been found to be more common than fellatio
in the relationships of adolescents (Newcomer & Udry, 1985).

Blumstein and Schwartz (1983) found that oral-genital sex sometimes can be the final act in the sexual episode, rather than one of
several foreplay behaviors. They found that heterosexual couples
who had more oral sex had less sexual intercourse. They also found
that gay couples were more likely than the other types of couples to
have oral sex while having sex. The percentage of couples who
usually or always have oral sex while they have sex was 50% for gay
couples, 39% for lesbian couples, and approximately 30% for heterosexual couples.

Anal Intercourse

> My favorite thing in sex with men is anal intercourse. It is most rewarding emotionally, although I feel somewhat strange admitting that. Because after the act is completed what I remember most vividly and savor long afterward was the union, the tenderness, and the language that was established between my partner and myself. Just being inside of a man makes us a unit and for that one moment of anal intercourse we are a complete "ONE" emotionally as well as physically. I love the feeling of his scrotum against mine. His manhood next to mine. (a man interviewed by Hite, 1981, p. 826)

Anal intercourse most often is associated with male homosexual couples. Blumstein and Schwartz (1983) found that 30% of their gay couples never or rarely had anal sex, 27% had it regularly with the partner and took turns being the penetrator, and 43% had it regularly but only one partner was the penetrator. The more sexually experienced gay men were more comfortable being penetrated, and the "strong, silent type" was more likely to be the penetrator.

Blumstein and Schwartz (1983) conducted their study before the AIDS crisis. Recent research conducted with gay men suggests that rates of anal intercourse have decreased. Gagnon (1990) wrote: "With the advent of AIDS and the recognition of the role of unprotected anal sex in HIV transmission, what has been observed is a dramatic decline (at least in those cities where competent research has been conducted) in both the general rates of anal sex and, in particular, the rate of unprotected anal sex" (p. 22).

Although anal sex is not often identified as a heterosexual practice, many heterosexual couples engage in penile penetration of the anus. Kinsey reported that 8% of his married sample had successfully experienced anal intercourse and that 3% had tried but were unsuccessful. The rates of anal intercourse were higher in the Hunt study. Hunt reported that approximately 25% of married couples under the age of 35 reported that they used anal intercourse occasionally and that about one-half of this age group had tried manual stimulation of the anus and one-fourth had engaged in anilingus, or oral stimulation of the anal area. From a review of several recent studies on sexuality, Voeller (1991) concluded that approximately 10% of American heterosexual couples engage in anal intercourse regularly.

Orgasms

> It is a very pleasurable sensation. All my tensions have really built to a peak and are suddenly released. It feels like a great upheaval; like all of the organs in the stomach area have turned over. It is extremely pleasurable. (p. 95)

> Orgasms gives me a feeling of unobstructed intensity of satisfaction. Accompanied with the emotional feeling and love one has for another, the reality of the sex drive, and our culturally conditioned status on sex, an orgasm is the only experience that sends my whole body and mind into a state of beautiful oblivion. (p. 95)

One of these descriptions of an orgasm was written by a man, and one by a woman (Vance & Wagner, 1976). Can you guess which is which? (Answers will appear later.)

Partners do not both experience orgasms *every* time they have sex. Males are more consistent in their experience of orgasms than females, and females, although they are less consistent, are more capable of multiple orgasms (Masters & Johnson, 1966). Both men and women occasionally fake orgasms, although women may do so more often (Darling, Davidson, & Cox, 1991; Hite, 1976, 1981).

Hunt (1974) reported that the wives in his study were having more orgasms than the wives in the Kinsey study. Women from the middle class report higher rates of orgasm than women from the working class (e.g., Hunt, 1974; Kinsey et al., 1948; Kinsey et al., 1953). Women say the factors that are most likely to inhibit them from having an orgasm are, in order of importance, lack of foreplay, fatigue, and preoccupation with nonsexual thoughts (Darling et al., 1991).

Homosexual and heterosexual couples may differ in how often they have orgasms, particularly when the comparison is between homosexual and heterosexual women. For example, Peplau et al. (1978) reported that 70% of the lesbians they studied almost always had orgasms in their current relationship, and only 4% never did. This rate of orgasm consistency is higher than that generally reported for heterosexual women. In another study, bisexual and lesbian women reported more orgasms per week than heterosexual women and also reported that the orgasms were more intense (Bressler & Lavender, 1986). Coleman et al. (1983) reported that a sample of lesbian women had more orgasms than a sample of hetero-sexual women. There are at least three reasons why lesbian women have greater orgasm consistency than heterosexual women (Coleman et al., 1983; Masters & Johnson, 1966): (a) Lesbians are likely to engage in those behaviors (e.g., oral-genital sex) that are most likely to result in orgasms, (b) a woman knows what is arousing to another woman; and (c) women may be able to communicate better with each other about what is pleasing.

(Oh, and by the way, the first quote above was written by a woman, and the second one was written by a man.)

Masturbation

I have more or less two sex lives, one with my wife and one with myself. I have masturbated for many years, but I now enjoy masturbation very much with no guilt (that I can consciously identify). I hope to discuss this with my wife someday, but free as I think I am with her, I can't bring myself to that point yet. I get pleasures that are deeply solitary, "forbidden" so to say, from masturbating, that are different from person-to-person lovemaking. I make love to myself. Most men won't admit that. But it's been a gradual lessening of guilt. I still have, in fact they're stronger, definite religious feelings. But I have now accommodated my religious feelings with my sexuality, and no area is more important here than masturbation. I find masturbation very healthy to my sexuality. I'm more in tune with my body and a better lover as a result of feeling freer, less guilt. (Hite, 1981, p. 564)

In many couples the partners engage in masturbation (solitary sexual activity) even if they are having an active sex life together. For example, Hunt (1974) reported that 72% of the husbands and 68% of the wives said they masturbated. High rates have been found in other studies of married couples and other close couples (e.g., Tavris & Sadd, 1977). Although some individuals may masturbate because they do not have sex in their relationship as frequently as they would like, no significant relation has been found between frequency of masturbation and frequency of sex with one's partner (Abramson, 1973); that is, partners who masturbate have sex with their partners about as often as partners who do not. Men masturbate more frequently than women, and most partners attempt to keep the masturbation a secret from each other (Grosskopf, 1983; Hessellund, 1976).

From the data from 38 married couples, Hessellund (1976) reported that a common place that spouses masturbate is in bed after the other has fallen asleep. Men, however, also like to do it in the bathroom. "The main difference between men and women here is that about 40 percent of the men always masturbate in the bathroom, either morning or night when they prepare for going to work or bed. Those men masturbate as a matter of routine before brushing their teeth and washing their hands. None of the wives states that this only takes place in the bathroom" (p. 137).

Variety in Sex

Some couples have sex at the same time, in the same place, and in the same way week after week. Other couples include more variety in their sexual script. Some also include devices. Sex toys, sexual aids, mirrors, video cameras, romantic novels, pornographic books, and X-rated movies are available for couples who want them.

Many years ago, it was almost always the husband in heterosexual marriages who suggested novel sexual activities or sexual aids. Hunt (1974) described how this had changed by the early 1970s: "Today the young wife is as likely as her husband to have heard and read about these and even far more fanciful novelties, thanks to the bumper crop of best-selling sexual manuals, candid magazine articles and erotic novels, and to the openness of talk about such things among her peers" (p. 182). This trend toward greater gender equality in "bringing home the ideas" most likely continues today. Work by Rubin (1976) with working-class couples, however, suggests that in these couples, husbands may be more likely than wives to push for more experimental sex. Consider the following quotes from her book *Worlds of Pain: Life in the Working-Class Family:*

> She thinks there's just one right position and one right way—in the dark with her eyes closed tight. Anything that varies from that makes her upset.
> —a husband (pp. 204-205)

Experimental? Oh, he's much more experimental than I am. Once in a while, I'll say, "Okay, you get a treat; we'll do it with the lights on." And I put the pillow over my head.
—a wife (p. 203)

To what degree is it important to contemporary couples that they try new sexual techniques? Kurdek (1991b) examined several aspects of sexuality in a sample consisting of both partners of 77 gay, 58 lesbian, 36 heterosexual cohabiting, and 49 heterosexual married couples. One aspect he examined was the importance of new sexual techniques. The men and women rated the importance of the following value: "Trying new sexual activities and techniques with my partner." On average, the couples rated this value moderately important. The mean or average on a 1 (*not important*) to 9 (*very important*) response scale ranged from 5.15 (for the lesbian couples) to 6.46 (for the gay couples).

From the recent telephone survey done with two national samples of married couples, Greeley (1991) reported on the kinds of sexual experimentation engaged in by married couples. He reported that more than one-half of couples in the sample said they experimented with new ways at least some of the time. Following is a list of activities he asked about and the percentage of respondents who said that they did each activity either "a lot" or "sometimes."

	A lot or sometimes
Abandon all of your sexual inhibitions	32%
Swim nude together	19%
Watch X-rated videos	21%
Buy erotic underclothes	20%
Make love outdoors	22%
Go to a hotel or motel to spend time alone with each other	34%
Take showers or baths together	39%

On the other hand, the same study found that 46% of married couples said they never "abandon all their sexual inhibitions," and only 7% said they abandon them a lot. Greeley (1991) wrote: "Are Americans more sexually inhibited than others? To that question we cannot give an answer. However, they are scarcely a sybaritic people. If there has been a revolution in the sexual relationships between husbands and wives, it still has a long way to go to produce a population of married men and women who are not seriously inhibited sexually" (p. 215).

❧ Sexual Satisfaction in Close Couples

We have discussed what couples *do* in their sex lives together. In this section we discuss what couples *feel* about the sexual aspect of their relationship. As an area of research, this is generally referred to as *sexual satisfaction*.

Measurement of Sexual Satisfaction

In many studies, particularly in the large-scale surveys, sexual satisfaction is assessed with a single global question. For example, in the telephone survey study conducted by the Gallup organization in the winter of 1989-1990 (see Greeley, 1991), respondents, who were married couples throughout the United States, were asked the following question: "How much satisfaction do you get out of your sexual relationship—a very great deal, a great deal, quite a bit, a fair amount, some, little, or none?" In the Blumstein and Schwartz (1983) study, respondents were asked how satisfied they were with several aspects of their relationship. One of the items listed was "our sex-life." A scale of 1 (*extremely satisfied*) to 9 (*not at all satisfied*) was provided. Although a single item has several advantages, including economy of space in a questionnaire, it has several disadvantages. First, it does not give the researcher much information. From a single item, the researcher is unable to learn which aspects of the sexual relationship are particularly satisfying. An individual is unlikely to be equally satisfied with all aspects of his or her sexual relationship. Second, a majority of respondents tend to place themselves at the high end of the response scale, although it is unlikely that all of these respondents are equally sexually satisfied with their relationship (Pinney, Gerrard, & Denney, 1987). In other words, there is very little *variation* in the responses. In defense of single items to measure sexual satisfaction, however, Greeley (1991) wrote:

> I know of no other way in which we can measure this satisfaction than by asking directly about it, save by interviewing God, who has

thus far been unavailable to both NORC and Gallup. Those who are prepared to wet their finger and hold it up to the wind are entitled to do so. Survey research, however great its limitations, is somewhat better than hearing voices in the night, reading auguries, conversing with one's friends, or self-analysis. (p. 69)

Some researchers, to overcome the problems of limited information and variation in single-item measures, have developed multiple-item scales to measure sexual satisfaction. One such scale is the Hudson, Harrison, and Crosscup (1981) Index of Sexual Satisfaction, a 25-item scale designed to measure degree of sexual discord or dissatisfaction with one's sexual relationship. The scale can be used in both therapy and research. Subjects respond to each of 25 items on a 1 (*rarely or none of the time*) to 5 (*most of the time*) response scale. Example items are "Sex is fun for my partner and me," "I enjoy the sex techniques that my partner likes or uses," "I feel that our sex life really adds a lot to our relationship," and "I feel that my sex life is boring" (this last item is reverse scored). Several other scales measure sexual satisfaction, including the Pinney Sexual Satisfaction Inventory (see Pinney et al., 1987), the LoPiccolo and Steger (1974) Sexual Interaction Inventory, and the Derogatis Sexual Functioning Inventory (Derogatis & Melisaratos, 1979). Furthermore, some scales designed to measure general marital or relationship satisfaction contain a subscale to measure sexual satisfaction or dissatisfaction (e.g., Snyder, 1979, 1981).

Other Subjective Assessments
Related to Sexuality

Although sexual satisfaction is the most commonly measured subjective assessment in the relationship, there are several related measures. Below we summarize several of these measures. For each, we pose a question for you, the reader, to consider concerning your own sexual relationship (or a possible future one).

1. Desire for Change in Sex: *How much do you want the sexuality in your relationship or your partner's sexual performance to be different?* Some scales measure the degree to which respondents wish their sexual relationship was different (the degree to which they desire

more or less of something). For example, one part of the Pinney Sexual Satisfaction Inventory (Pinney et al., 1987) contains items that begin "I wish . . . ." Some of the items included in the scale are "I wish my partner(s) were more loving and caring when we make love," "I wish my partner(s) initiated sex more often," and "I wish my partner(s) could communicate more openly about what he/she wants in our sexual relationship." For other examples of research measuring desires for changes in the sexual relationship, see Denny, Field, and Quadagno (1984), Halpern and Sherman (1979), and Hatfield, Sprecher, Pillemer, Greenberger, and Wexler (1988).

2. Sexual Desire: *How much do you desire to have sex with your partner?* Surprisingly, sexual desire has been examined infrequently within the context of the close relationship. Hurlbert (1991) asked married women to rate their interest in participating in each of several sexual activities with their husbands on a 1 (*extremely low*) to 10 (*extremely high*) basis. (See also Hurlbert & Whittaker, 1991.) McCabe (1987) surveyed young adults about whether they *desire* sexual intercourse at different stages of dating.

3. Sexual Arousability: *How aroused do you become in response to sexual activities with your partner?* Hoon, Hoon, and Wincze (1976) developed a Sexual Arousability Inventory to measure people's perception of their sexual arousability in response to 28 erotic experiences. Most of the acts in the scale refer to sexual behaviors with a loved one (e.g., "When you see a loved one nude," "When you caress a loved one's genitals with your fingers," "When a loved one kisses you with an exploring tongue").

4. Importance of Sex: *How important is sex to your relationship?* In a few studies respondents have been asked how important sex is to their relationship. For example, the couples in the Boston Dating Couples Study were asked to rate how important "desire for sexual activity" was as a dating goal. In a study on marital sexuality, Schenk, Pfrang, and Rausche (1983) included a 4-item scale to measure *the importance of sexuality.* For example, one item referred to the importance of sexual intercourse with the marital partner.

5. Sexual Compatibility: *How sexually compatible are you and your partner?* This concept generally refers to the degree that two people

are similar in their sexual needs. Blumstein and Schwartz (1983) asked their respondents one direct question concerning how *compatible* their sexual relationship was. In a recent book, Barbach and Geisinger (1992) presented a 50-item scale designed to measure the degree to which relationship partners are compatible and are likely to have a chance at success in the relationship. Some of the items refer to sexual compatibility and include "My partner understands my sexual needs and satisfies them," "I feel relaxed and sexually uninhibited with my partner," and "I like the way my partner looks, smells, tastes, and feels." In some studies, couples also have been asked about how much they disagree about sex.

Some researchers might argue that all of the above measures are too subjective. For example, Hunt (1974) wrote: "Unfortunately, most measurements of sexual pleasure and satisfaction with marital sex life must rely on subjective and imprecise self-evaluations. What one individual means when he or she says that his or her married sex life is 'very pleasurable' may be very different from what another individual means by the same term" (p. 207). Hunt used the occurrence of an *orgasm* as an objective indicator of sexual satisfaction (particularly for women). Two other more objective, but indirect, measures of the quality of the sex in the relationship might be the occurrence of *sexual dysfunctions* and of *extradyadic sexual relationships*. It can be presumed that at least some dysfunctions (e.g., erectile difficulties, painful intercourse) and at least some extradyadic affairs occur because one or both partners are sexually dissatisfied in their primary relationship.

How Sexually Satisfied Are Couples Today?

Couples today seem to be relatively satisfied with the sexual aspect of their relationship, at least as indicated by single-item measures (but keep in mind that people tend to respond at the high end of such response scales). In his recent study of intimacy and love, conducted with probability samples of American couples (by the Gallup organization), Greeley (1991) found that approximately one-third of the husbands and wives reported "a very great deal" of satisfaction, and another one-third reported "a great deal" of satisfaction. In a study of 50 professional couples, Brown and Auerback (1981) reported that 88% of the men and 66% of the women were very pleased with the sexual aspect of their life. Several other studies also have shown that couples are moderately to highly sexually satisfied in their relationships (see Blumstein & Schwartz, 1983; Fisher, 1973; and Peplau et al., 1978).

Some studies have compared the satisfaction reported for the sexual aspect of the relationship with the satisfaction reported for other areas of the relationship. For example, Rhyne (1981) asked more than 2,000 married Canadians how satisfied they were with nine aspects of their marriage: love, interest, help at home, treatment by in-laws, time spent at home, spouse's friends, spouse's time with children, friendship, and sexual gratification. Of these nine areas in the relationship, both men and women were most satisfied with the sexual gratification in the marriage. Women reported slightly more satisfaction than men with sexual gratification, although men were more satisfied than women in all of the other areas. Fisher (1973), in his study of women's sexual responses, asked a sample of middle-class wives to rank order various life events in terms of their enjoyment. Sexual intercourse was ranked as the most enjoyable event, more enjoyable than such activities as eating, sleeping, and watching television. Of course, it could be argued that sex would be ranked lower in a list that included other sorts of activities. The list did not include "touching and cuddling," which seems to be very important to women. Some readers of this book will remember that, in 1985, Ann Landers asked her readers: "Would you be content to be held close and treated tenderly and forget about 'the act'?" More than 90,000 women responded, and 72% said they preferred the cuddling part over "the act" (Angier, 1985).

If we look at some of the other indicators of sexual satisfaction, as reviewed above, we find less sexually harmonious relationships. For example, Masters and Johnson (1970) estimated that 50% of American married couples currently have or will develop some type of sexual dysfunction. Research also suggests that many couples experience one or both partners having an extradyadic relationship. Kinsey and his colleagues (1948, 1953) found that 50% of the men and 26% of the women in their study had an extramarital affair by the age of 45. Blumstein and Schwartz (1983) reported that the rates of nonmonogamy were 26% for married males, 21% for married females, 33% for male cohabitors, 30% for female cohabitors, 82% for gay men, and 28% for lesbians.

Which Types of Couples
Are More Sexually Satisfied?

Not all couples are equally satisfied with the sexual aspect of their relationship. Although working-class and middle-class couples may engage in the same kinds of sexual behaviors (Hunt, 1974; Rubin, 1976), the working-class wives have been found to be more uncomfortable about some of the behaviors they engage in, particularly oral-genital sex (Rubin, 1976). Other evidence indicates that middle-class couples may be more sexually satisfied than lower-class couples (e.g., Kinsey et al., 1948; Kinsey et al., 1953; Rainwater, 1966), although not all evidence has shown this difference (e.g., Hudson et al., 1981). Younger couples also may be more satisfied than older couples. For example, Greeley (1991) found that sexual satisfaction was negatively associated with the age of the spouse. Whereas over 80% of the respondents in their 20s reported very great satisfaction, this measure was approximately 25% for those 70 years of age. In one study, however, middle-age married adults reported that they enjoyed sex more at the current time than they did earlier in the marriage (Brown & Auerback, 1981).

Different couple types also have been compared on sexual satisfaction. Kurdek (1991b) compared the sexual satisfaction of four types of couples: gay, lesbian, heterosexual unmarried, and heterosexual married. Sexual satisfaction was measured by four items (an example item: "I enjoy my sexual relationship with my partner"). No differences were found among the four types of couples on sexual satisfaction. Other evidence, however, has suggested that homosexuals may be more satisfied with the sex in their close relationships than heterosexuals (Coleman et al., 1983; Masters & Johnson, 1979).

Box 4.2 summarizes other individual factors, including personality characteristics, that have been found to be associated with sexual satisfaction. In the next section we discuss how sexual behaviors are related to sexual satisfaction. Then, in the next chapter, we discuss relationship factors associated with sexual satisfaction.

BOX 4.2

*Individual and Personality Factors Associated
With Sexual Satisfaction*

—holding nontraditional attitudes toward women's roles (Kirkpatrick, 1980)
—having positive attitudes about one's body (Perlman & Abramson, 1982)
—having positive attitudes about the partner's body, particularly for men (Margolin & White, 1987)

—being both Irish and Catholic (Greeley, 1991)
—characterizing oneself as "living in the here and now" (Paxton & Turner, 1978; Waterman, Chiauzzi, & Gruenbaum, 1979)
—being extroverted (Schenk et al., 1983)
—being sexually assertive, for women (Hurlbert, 1991)

---

*How Sexual Satisfaction Is Associated
With Sexual Behaviors*

Certain patterns of sexual behaviors are associated with sexual satisfaction. Why do such patterns exist? There are three basic possibilities:

1. Couples who engage in particular behaviors (e.g., oral-genital sex) may come to be more sexually satisfied than couples who do not engage in these behaviors.
2. Couples who are initially sexually satisfied are more likely to engage in certain sexual behaviors (e.g., oral-genital sex) than couples who are not sexually satisfied.
3. Another factor, such as a personality characteristic or a quality of the relationship, may affect both sexual satisfaction and sexual behavior.

Most often, it is assumed that the first possibility (certain behaviors bring more satisfaction) is operating, but the reader should be aware that the association found between sexual satisfaction and sexual behaviors also can be explained by one or both of the other two causal directions.

Sexual Frequency

> It is also said that the general sexual satisfaction of a sexual relationship doesn't depend on how frequently the spouses make love. The hell it doesn't! (Greeley, 1991, p. 68)

In his national sample of married couples, Greeley (1991) found that the frequency of sex was a strong predictor of sexual satisfaction. For example, of those who said they have sex at least once per week, 43% reported a high level of sexual satisfaction, whereas only 17% of those who said they have sex less than once per week scored at the high end of this measure. Blumstein and Schwartz (1983) found that, for all couple types in their study (gay, lesbian, and heterosexual), sexual frequency was positively correlated with a measure of sexual quality or satisfaction. Even after other variables were controlled (e.g., duration of the relationship, educational level), the two variables were correlated around .50. Several other studies also have found that sexual frequency and sexual satisfaction or pleasure are positively related (e.g., Hunt, 1974; Levin & Levin, 1975; Peplau et al., 1978; Pinney et al., 1987; Trussell & Westoff, 1980). Furthermore, a positive association has been found between frequency of oral-genital sex and sexual satisfaction (Blumstein & Schwartz, 1983).

Particular Sexual Acts

Two of the most intimate sexual acts are sexual intercourse and oral-genital sex. Blumstein and Schwartz (1983) examined how sexual intercourse and oral-genital sex are each related to sexual satisfaction in the relationship. These researchers described the effect of sexual intercourse on sexual satisfaction in heterosexual couples in the following way: "We discover that intercourse is just one sexual act among others that heterosexual men enjoy—but a central ingredient in women's happiness" (p. 227). This statement may seem contrary to the finding that men desire sexual intercourse to a greater degree than women (Denney et al., 1984). As explained by Blumstein and Schwartz (1983), however, the greater association between sexual intercourse and sexual satisfaction for women than for men is not because women find intercourse to be more physically satisfying than men do, but because it is a sexual act that involves both partners equally and thus women may feel more intimate with this act than with others.

A reverse gender difference was found for the relationship between oral-genital sex and sexual satisfaction; that is, Blumstein and Schwartz (1983) found that oral sex was more important for the satisfaction of heterosexual men than for the satisfaction of heterosexual women. More specifically, heterosexual men who received and/or gave oral sex were happier with their sex life than men who were not having oral sex. For heterosexual women, however, oral sex was not related to their sexual satisfaction.

What about homosexual couples? Oral sex was related to sexual satisfaction in both lesbian and gay couples. Hence oral sex is linked to sexual satisfaction more for lesbian women than for heterosexual women.

Orgasms

Whereas men tend to have orgasms consistently, women do not. Hence we can ask whether, for women, having orgasms is associated with sexual satisfaction. Results indicate that this is the case. For example, Pinney et al. (1987) found, in a sample of young women, that of 11 possible predictors of sexual satisfaction, the second strongest predictor was orgasm consistency (measured by the percentage of sexual interaction where the woman experiences orgasm). Other research also has found that female orgasm consistency is related to sexual satisfaction in both heterosexual (Kirkpatrick, 1980; Perlman & Abramson, 1982) and lesbian relationships (Peplau et al., 1978).

It may be not only the occurrence of orgasm that is related to women's sexual satisfaction but also the *timing* of the orgasm. In a study of 709 heterosexually active, professional nurses, Darling et al. (1991) found that women who experienced their orgasm *after* their partner did reported less sexual satisfaction than subjects who experienced it before or at about the same time. You may be curious about how many women were classified into each of these groups: Of the 709 nurses, 45% said they had orgasm before, 19% said they had orgasm at about the same time, and 36% said they had orgasm after their partner did.

Masturbation

Relationship partners who masturbate are not necessarily more sexually dissatisfied than relationship partners who do not masturbate. In general, no relation has been found between frequency of masturbation and satisfaction with one's relationship (e.g., Jensen, 1978). In one study conducted with women, masturbation actually was associated with greater sexual satisfaction. Hurlbert and Whittaker (1991) sorted a sample of married women into two groups: those who had masturbated to orgasm and those who had not. Women who masturbated, relative to those who did not, scored higher on a sexual satisfaction scale, on desire for sexual activity with the spouse, and on several other variables as well (e.g., marital satisfaction).

Experimentation in Sex

Couples who vary their routine in having sex may be more likely to be satisfied with their sex together than couples who do not. For example, Greeley (1991) found that those who reported being experimental in their lovemaking were more likely to be sexually satisfied.

❧ Summary

This chapter focused on sex in more developed close relationships (e.g., marriage). We first summarized the literature on how often couples have sex. Couples tend to have sex frequently early in their relationship (or marriage), but this frequency often declines with length of time in the relationship and increasing ages of the partners. We also considered the variety of behaviors (e.g., kissing, oral-genital sex) that might be included in a couple's sexual script. Then we considered the sexual satisfaction of couples and the factors (e.g., types of behaviors engaged in, background factors) associated with quality of sex in a relationship.

In the next chapter, we examine how two important aspects of sexuality reviewed in this chapter—sexual frequency and sexual satisfaction—are associated with several other aspects of the relationship.

5

Sexuality and Other Dimensions of the Close Relationship

The sexual part of a close relationship, although important to the overall relationship, is still only one aspect of it. In this chapter we discuss how sexuality in the relationship is related to other important dimensions of the relationship. This chapter is divided into three sections. First, we discuss how sexuality (especially the sexual act) can be considered as one element among several that characterize close relationships; that is, we address the major question, What are couples expressing when they have sex? Second, we address the question, How does sexuality in the relationship affect other dimensions of the relationship, such as satisfaction and love? Furthermore, do these other dimensions have an impact on sexuality? We also discuss whether sexuality has an influence on whether couples stay together or break up. Finally, we discuss communication and sexuality in close relationships: Who initiates sex and how? How is communication about sexuality related to sexual satisfaction?

ᴥ Sex as One Element in the Close Relationship

In a close relationship, sex is more than a physical act. When two bodies belonging to two intertwined lives join in an act of sex, much more than physical sensations gets expressed. In this section we consider higher order constructs that have been identified by relationship researchers as important to understanding behaviors in close relationships. Having sex is one aspect of each of these higher order constructs or approaches in close relationships (see Figure 5.1).

Sex as an Act of Self-Disclosure

Self-disclosure is the process by which one person reveals personal information about him- or herself to another person. Self-disclosure is a major facet of the close relationship. As two people become close, they tend to reveal more and more aspects of themselves (e.g., Altman & Taylor, 1973; Derlega & Berg, 1987).

All of the actions that typically occur in the sex act—being nude in front of one's partner, expressing to the partner what feels good, actually having sex, experiencing an orgasm—are considered to be very intimate self-disclosures. Reiss (1989), a sociologist, argued that sexuality is valued universally, in part, because it is a form of self-disclosure: "Experiencing intense physical pleasure in the presence of another person reveals parts of oneself which are not generally known even by one's close friends. Sexual partners thus reveal their emotions and responses in their sexual interactions and thereby learn more about each other" (p. 10).

Sex as an Act of Intimacy

Sex is also a way to be intimate with another. *Intimacy* has been defined as a feeling of closeness and sharing of emotional and physical experiences with another person (e.g., Schaefer & Olson, 1981). Researchers have found that people assume that sexuality is an impor-

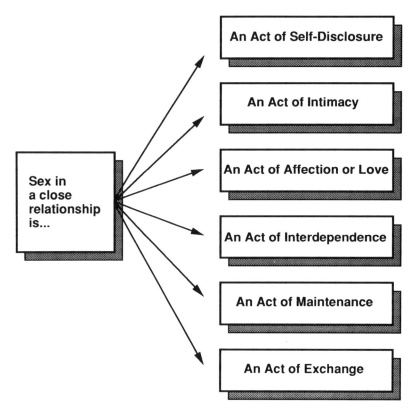

Figure 5.1. Sex as One Element in the Close Relationship

tant part of intimacy. For example, Waring, Tillman, Frelick, Russell, and Weisz (1980) asked adults, "What does intimacy mean to you?" Sexuality and affection were among the major themes that emerged from the subjects' responses.

Several scales have been developed to measure intimacy, and most of them contain items to measure sexual intimacy or physical expression. In their Personal Assessment of Intimacy in Relationships (PAIR) Inventory, Schaefer and Olson (1981) measured five aspects of intimacy in a close relationship. One type of intimacy is *sexual* (sharing affection and sexual activity), assessed by items such as "Sexual expression is an essential part of our relationship" and

"I am satisfied with our sex life." The other four types of intimacy are *emotional* (experiencing a closeness of feelings), *social* (sharing friends), *intellectual* (sharing ideas), and *recreational* (sharing interests and hobbies). Other intimacy scales that include items to measure a sexual dimension of the relationship are the Waring Intimacy Scale (e.g., Reddon, Patton, & Waring, 1985; Waring, McElrath, Lefcoe, & Weisz, 1981) and the Psychosocial Intimacy Questionnaire (Tesch, 1985).

Sex as an Act of Affection or Love

As noted in Chapter 3, when intimate partners are asked why they have sex with their partner (particularly the first time), reasons given include expressions of love and affection (e.g., Carroll et al., 1985; Christopher & Cate, 1984). Couples who have been together for many years continue to have sex to express love. Thus sex with one's partner can be considered an expression of love and affection and is similar to such behaviors as sending flowers, saying "I love you," giving gifts, and making chicken soup when the partner feels ill.

Buss (1989b) called these kinds of behaviors *love acts*, which he referred to as "overt manifestation or actions that have tangible consequences" (p. 100). In one study, he asked 100 subjects to respond to the following:

> Please think of people you know of your own gender (sex) who have been or are currently in love. With these individuals in mind, write down five acts or behaviors that they have performed (or might perform) that reflect or exemplify their love. Be sure to write down acts or behaviors. An act is something that a person does or did, not something that they are. (p. 110)

Subjects then were asked to name love acts for people of the opposite sex. Buss found that sex was one of the love acts most frequently mentioned by the subjects—19% of the sample mentioned it. A gender difference emerged in how frequently sex was identified as a love act. Whereas only 8% of the females mentioned sex as a love act, 32% of the males did so.

On the basis of the acts identified in the first study, Buss (1989b) generated a list of 100 love acts for a second study. Two example acts were: "He made love to her" and "He took care of her when she was sick." Subjects then were asked to rate how good each act was as an example of love. Half of the subjects rated the love acts for a male, and half rated them for a female. Of the 40 acts (out of 100) judged by the subjects to be most prototypical of love, two referred to sexual intimacy: "She (he) spent the night with him (her)" and "He (she) made love to her (him)." These two sexual acts, however, were rated as less prototypical of love than many other types of acts, such as "She (he) agreed to marry him (her)" and "She (he) listened devotedly to his (her) problems." The males in the second study were also more likely than the females to see sex acts as love acts.

Sex as an Act of Interdependence

As two people become close and engage in more activities together, they become more interdependent. Kelley et al. (1983) defined *high interdependence* in the following way:

> A high degree of interdependence between two people is revealed in four properties of their interconnected activities: (1) the individuals have *frequent* impact on each other; (2) the degree of impact per each occurrence is *strong;* (3) the impact involves *diverse* kinds of activities for each person; and (4) all of these properties characterize the interconnected activity series for a relatively long *duration* of time. (p. 13)

One way that partners can be interdependent is by depending on each other for sexual activity. Berscheid, Snyder, and Omoto (1989) created a scale—the Closeness Inventory—to measure relationship interdependence or closeness. To assess the diversity dimension from the definition above, they presented subjects with a list of activities and asked them to check all of the activities they had done alone with the partner during the previous week. One activity is "engaged in sexual relations." Examples of other activities included in the list are "prepared a meal," "visited friends," "attended a sporting event," and "discussed things of a personal nature."

Omoto, Berscheid, and Snyder (1987) suggested that being interdependent in the sexual area is associated with being interdependent in other areas of the relationship. They compared participants involved in romantic, nonsexual relationships (defined as not having had sex in the previous week) with participants involved in romantic, sexual relationships (having had sex in the previous week) on several measures. One measure was the section of the Closeness Inventory that asked about the number of times they had engaged in each of 37 activities during the previous week either alone, alone with the partner, with the partner in the presence of others, or with people other than the partner. The sexually involved respondents reported doing a greater number and more different types of activities with their partner during the previous week than the sexually noninvolved respondents. Compared with the respondents who were sexually active, those who were not sexually involved reported more activities with people other than the partner. Sexually involved respondents also expressed greater dependency on and emotional attachment to their partner. The authors concluded: "Simply put, *sexual activity made a difference,* with sexual status related *quantitatively* to behaviors *within* the relationship (with the partner) and to behaviors *outside* of the relationship (with others)" (p. 7). In other ways, however, the two groups were very similar. No differences were found in feelings of insecurity, in estimates of closeness, and in loving and liking for partner.

Sex as an Act of Maintenance

Once a close relationship develops, partners must engage in behaviors to help maintain the relationship. Several researchers in the close relationships field recently have begun to study and measure *maintenance strategies*—that is, the common strategies that couples use to maintain their relationships. In some of this theoretical and empirical work, physical or sexual affection is identified as one type of maintenance strategy. For example, Bell, Daly, and Gonzalez (1987) identified 28 potential maintenance strategies, and one of these was physical affection. It was operationalized as frequency of sexual relations. Dindia (1988) identified the category of romantic strategies, and included among the specific examples were sex and physical affection. Dainton (1991) modified a typology developed by Stafford and Canary (1991) and added physical affection. According to this line of research, then, sexual and/or physical expression is one strategy that couples use to maintain their relationship.

Sex as an Act of Exchange

> He gets different treats at different times, depending on what he deser-
> ves. Sometimes I let him do that oral stuff you're talking about to me.
> Sometimes when he's very good, I do it to him. (a woman interviewed
> by Rubin, 1976, p. 207)

The woman quoted above recognized the exchange value of sex. Exchange is pervasive in intimate relationships. Sex can be considered one of many exchange elements in close relationships; that is, partners in a relationship exchange a variety of resources, and within this exchange one partner's sexual favors may be exchanged for the other's sexual favors and/or for other types of rewards in the relationship (e.g., love, gifts). In some recent research, for example, researchers have asked intimate partners how much they receive from the relationship in several different areas. A list of seven resources that has been used in several research studies consists of love, status, services, information, goods, money, and sex (Cate, Lloyd, Henton, & Larson, 1982; Michaels, Acock, & Edwards, 1986). (Sex was added to the list of six resources originally identified by Foa and Foa [1974].) Safilios-Rothschild (1976) also argued that both love and sex are major resources exchanged in the intimate relationship.

The Association Between Sexuality and Other Important Dimensions of the Relationship

What a couple does in their sex life together and how they feel about what they do is likely to affect how they feel about each other more generally and how they behave toward each other in nonsexual situations. Furthermore, the nonsexual aspects of the relationship are also likely to impact the sexual aspect. In this section of the chapter, we examine how the degree and frequency of sex and sexual satisfaction are related to other important dimensions of the relationship. Figure 5.2 presents a diagram of the variables considered in this section. We look at general relationship satisfaction, love, conflict, and equity. We have chosen these variables because they have been examined most frequently in conjunction with sexuality, but they certainly do not represent an exhaustive list of relationship dimensions related to sexuality. As you can see from the diagram, we believe that these other relationship dimensions both affect and are affected by the sexuality in the close relationship. At the end of this section, we discuss how sexuality in the relationship affects whether the relationship endures over time.

General Relationship Satisfaction

The Relationship Between Incidence of or Frequency of Sex and Relationship Satisfaction

The research examining the relationship between sexual activity and relationship satisfaction among dating couples has focused on whether premarital couples who have sex are more satisfied overall than premarital couples who have not had sex (the effect of the incidence or occurrence of sexual behavior). As we discussed earlier in this book, Peplau et al. (1977), in the Boston Dating Couples Study, identified three types of couples: couples who had sex early in the relationship (within the first month), couples who had sex later (about the sixth month), and couples who abstained from sex. These three groups of couples did not differ in their levels of overall relationship satisfaction.

Research conducted with more committed couples has focused on how sexual frequency is related to the overall satisfaction or happiness with the relationship. For example, Blumstein and Schwartz (1983) described the relationship they found between sexual frequency and relationship satisfaction for married couples in the following way: "Married couples feel so strongly about having sex often that those who say they have it with their partner infrequently tend to be dissatisfied with their entire relationship" (p. 201). The quantity of sex also was found to be important to the overall quality of the relationships for gay men and male cohabitors, but not for lesbians and female cohabitors. Other studies also have found frequency of sex to be significantly related to overall relationship happiness or satisfaction (e.g., Birchler & Webb, 1977; Buss, Study 3, 1989a).

Does frequency of sex cause the level of relationship satisfaction, or does the level of relationship satisfaction cause frequency of sex?

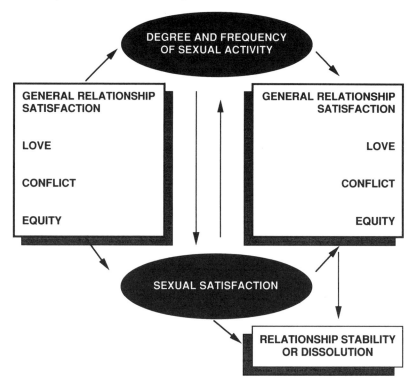

Figure 5.2. Relationship Between Sexuality and Other Dimensions of the Close Relationship

Blumstein and Schwartz (1983) addressed the issue of the causal direction between these variables:

> It is hard to know whether an unsatisfactory relationship leads to less frequent sexual activity and reduced sexual pleasure or whether the problems begin in the bedroom and eventually corrode the entire relationship. From our vantage point it looks as if other problems come into the bedroom and make it less likely that the couple will want to have sex together. The low frequency then becomes a source of dissatisfaction in and of itself. (p. 201)

Not all studies, however, have found a significant relationship between frequency of sex and relationship satisfaction, particularly when other variables are controlled. For example, Greeley (1991) found that frequency of sex did not affect overall relationship quality once sexual satisfaction was controlled. His results suggest that quantity of sex affects overall relationship satisfaction indirectly through its effect on sexual satisfaction; that is, frequency of sex increases sexual satisfaction, which then increases relationship satisfaction. Another study suggests that sexual frequency may make an important contribution to relationship satisfaction only insofar as it is considered to be a form of affectional expression. Huston and Vangelisti (1991) separated the effects of sexual frequency (or sexual interest) from affectional expression and found that affectional expression positively affected marital satisfaction. In a very early study that examined the relationship between sexual frequency and relationship satisfaction, Terman, Buttenweiser, Ferguson, Johnson, and Wilson (1938) found that the discrepancy between desired and actual frequency of sex was the most important predictor of marital satisfaction. Individuals who were having sex about as often as they wanted to were satisfied with their marriage. Those who were not, were dissatisfied.

The Relationship Between Sexual Satisfaction and Relationship Satisfaction

Sexual satisfaction also is related to general relationship satisfaction. In fact, as stated above, the effects of sexual frequency may be mediated through sexual satisfaction. Research shows an association between satisfaction with the sexual aspect of the relationship and satisfaction with the overall relationship. Hunt (1974) found a strong association between the extent to which husbands and wives found the sexual aspect of their relationship satisfying and the level of marital closeness or satisfaction. More specifically, couples who rated their marriage as very close emotionally rated marital sexual intercourse as highly pleasurable, while 60% of women and 40% of men who rated their marriage as not close evaluated sexual intercourse as unpleasurable. Data from a *Redbook* survey also indicate an association between sexual satisfaction and relationship satisfaction. Of the women who reported happy marriages, 80% also said their sex life was good. Conversely, 70% of women who described their marriage as poor also reported a poor sex life (Tavris & Sadd, 1977). Greeley (1991) found that sexual satisfaction was a contributing factor to marital happiness, even after controlling for other factors. Other research also shows a positive relationship between sexual satisfaction and relationship satisfaction (e.g., Rhyne, 1981; Schenk et al., 1983).

Love

In our society, love and sexuality are closely linked. As we discussed in Chapter 1, people believe that sex is most acceptable in a loving relationship. Aron and Aron (1991) stated, "This attitude is saying that love is primary and sex must wait for it" (p. 38). We also discussed in Chapter 3 how intimate partners, particularly females, say they are motivated to have sex in order to express love to their partner. Other research (e.g., Brown & Auerback, 1981) shows that intimate partners who have been together for years continue to be motivated to have sex for love reasons. In this section we further consider the relationship between love and sex but focus on love felt directly for a partner (rather than attitudes about love or love as a motive for sex). We address the questions, Does the *degree* of love experienced between relationship partners affect their sexual intimacy? and Are some *types* of love more associated with sexual intimacy than other types? Most of the research addressing these questions has been conducted with dating couples.

Love and Sex Go Together

Research indicates that the amount of love experienced for one's dating partner is positively related to the level of sexual intimacy in the relationship. For example, in their study of university students and college-age nonstudents, DeLamater and MacCorquodale (1979) found that the individuals who were more emotionally attached or in love reported greater sexual involvement in the relationship. This does not mean, however, that dating partners who wait to have sex love each other any less than those who have sex early in the relationship. Peplau et al. (1977) examined the relationship between the level of sexual behavior and the emotional intimacy of the relationship.

They found that the couples who had sex late in the relationship (average of 6 months after they started going out together), relative to those couples who had sex early in the relationship, were more likely to say they were "in love" with each other, to score higher on Rubin's (1970) Love Scale, to feel closer to their partner, and to be more likely to expect to marry their partner. The researchers reported that two processes might explain this link between later sex and greater love. First, later-sex couples may delay sexual intercourse until the relationship is emotionally close. Second, later-sex couples, when they engage in sex, may interpret this behavior in the context of love feelings, whereas early-sex couples, who are more liberal in their attitudes, may interpret their sexual behavior in erotic terms.

Other research also suggests that the link between love and sex may be stronger at more committed stages of the relationship. Christopher and Cate (1988) examined the degree to which love and other relationship dimensions predicted level of sexual expression in a group of dating couples. The dating individuals completed measures about their relationship (e.g., love) and about the level of sexual involvement for four previous stages of dating: first date, casually dating, when they were considering becoming a couple, and when they identified themselves as a couple with a monogamous commitment to the relationship. The level of sexual involvement in the relationship was measured by Bentler's (1968a, 1968b) Heterosexual Assessment Scale, which asks about 21 different sexual behaviors. The researchers examined how the level of sexual intimacy at each of the relationship stages was predicted by love and other relationship dimensions at the previous stages. Love was found to be associated with a high level of sexual intimacy, but particularly at the stage when the dating individuals were considering becoming a couple.

Feelings of love between spouses also may affect the degree to which they want to have frequent sex. Edwards and Booth (1976) examined how several variables that described the marriage might affect how frequently spouses have sex. Of the marital variables considered, the perception that the partner was as loving as he or she used to be was the strongest predictor of frequent sexual intercourse.

Types of Love

A great deal of research conducted in the past two decades shows that there is not just one type of love or one way of loving a partner. Social psychologists have identified several types of love. It has been suggested, although infrequently examined, that these different types of love may be related to sexuality in the relationship in different ways.

To illustrate this idea, we focus on the early distinction made between passionate love and companionate love. *Passionate love* has been defined as "A state of intense longing for union with another. Reciprocated love (union with the other) is associated with fulfillment and ecstasy. Unrequited love (separation) with emptiness; with anxiety and despair. A state of intense physiological arousal" (Hatfield & Walster, 1978, p. 9). *Companionate love,* on the other hand, is defined by these same authors as "the affection we feel for those with whom our lives are deeply entwined" (p. 9). Brehm (1985) speculated on the role of sexuality in each of these types of love.

> Passionate love often involves very intense sexual experiences that may be quite frequent. However, it is also possible for romantic lovers to have very little sexual contact or even none at all. No matter what the actual sexual interaction, passionate love feels highly sexualized: the person who is passionately in love is strongly sexually attracted to the partner.
>
> In contrast, companionate love can be experienced without either sexual interaction or sexualized feelings—as, for example, in a close, but nonsexual friendship. Companionate love relationships, however, often do include sexual activity that is both frequent and enjoyable, but usually not of the intensity found in the sexual interactions of passionate love partners. (p. 93)

Hatfield and Sprecher (1986a) developed a scale to measure passionate love and reported that, in dating relationships, their scale was positively correlated with sexual satisfaction and sexual excitement, with the desire to engage in sex with the partner, and with the desire to be held and kissed by the partner. Although they did not examine whether passionate love is more correlated with sexual interest and desire than is companionate love, another study provided indirect evidence that this might be the case. Rabehl, Ridge, and Berscheid (1992) distinguished between "loving" someone and "being in love" with someone. They argued that most people can understand the distinction between these two terms ("I love you, but I am not in love with you"). This distinction may be similar to the distinction between passionate ("I'm in love with you") and companionate ("I love you") love. Their two studies showed that students assume a person presented as "in love" experiences more sexual desire and sexual attraction for a partner than a person who "loves." They concluded: "Thus, our findings suggest that although sexuality may not be a central feature of love, it is most definitely a central feature of the state of being in love" (p. 24).

The findings from another study also suggest that being in love is a highly sexual state. In his national study of married couples, Greeley (1991) identified different stages of marriage. The first stage he called "falling in love." Seventeen percent of the total sample (but 47% of those in their first year of marriage) placed themselves in the falling in love phase. Greeley described the falling in love stage in the following way:

> When one is in love, one is absorbed, preoccupied, tense and intense, and filled with a sexual longing which permeates the rest of existence, making it both glorious and exhausting. . . . Feeling that you're in love with your spouse correlates with (and probably is both a cause of and an effect of) a very different kind of sexual and interpersonal life than that reported by other Americans. Those who are falling in love seem truly to be by love possessed. (pp. 122-124)

Although being passionately in love may be a desirable state to be in, in part because of the heightened sexual feelings, it also has a negative side: There is emotional upheaval, uncertainty, and fear.

Conflict

Although we might like to believe that intimate partners are only happy with each other and never fight or have conflicts, we know this is not true. Couples argue and have conflict, and this conflict can be related to the sexuality in the relationship. As shown in our model in Figure 5.2, conflict (or harmony, its opposite) can occur as a consequence of the level of sexual activity and sexual pleasure

use erotic words (e.g., make love, fuck, suck, jack off, stroke) to enhance sexual arousal in either themselves or their partner.

Wells (1990) explored what terminology was erotic or arousing for men and women, and comparisons also were made between homosexuals and heterosexuals. The researchers asked undergraduate students (obtained from classes and from the gay-lesbian organization on campus) to write the word (if any) they would use with a spouse or lover for each of the following: male genitalia, female genitalia, coitus, oral-genital contact, and hand-genital contact. Lesbians and gay men were more likely than heterosexual men and women to say that they would use erotic or arousing terms with a lover and were more likely to talk to their partner about sexual activity.

Couples may develop their own pet names for genitalia and their own special terms for sexual activities ("personal idioms"), which can enhance feelings of closeness and love in the relationship (e.g., Bell, Buerkel-Rothfuss, & Gore, 1987; Cornog, 1986).

Initiation and Acceptance or Refusal of Sex

In Chapter 3 we noted that men are more likely than women to initiate the first sexual contacts in a developing relationship. Although we would expect to find greater equality in sexual initiation within committed relationships, research suggests that men continue to initiate sex more often than women, even after several years of being together.

Blumstein and Schwartz (1983) asked the respondents in their study who was more likely to "let the other know one would like to have sex." Of the husbands, 51% said they were more likely to initiate sex, 33% said the initiation was equal, and 16% said the partner was more likely to initiate sex. Of the wives, 12% said they were more likely to initiate sex, 40% said the initiation was equal, and 48% said the partner was more likely to initiate sex. A greater percentage of the cohabitors reported that sexual initiation was equal in their relationship (42% of male cohabitors, 46% of female cohabitors), but even in cohabiting relationships, men were more likely to do the sexual initiating.

Byers and Heinlein (1989) had married and cohabiting individuals keep a record of their sexual interactions over a 1-week period.

Male partners were found to initiate sex more often than female partners. Furthermore, more than twice as many women (23%) as men (10%) did not initiate sex during the week of the study. In her study of working-class couples, Rubin (1976) also found that wives hesitated to take the initiative in sex. Some of these women did not initiate sex because they did not want to be accused of being non-feminine. For example, one working-class wife interviewed by Rubin stated: "I don't like to think he might think I was being aggressive, so I don't usually make any suggestions. Most of the time it's okay because he can usually tell when I'm in the mood. But if he can't, I just wait" (p. 210).

Although men, in general, initiate sexual activity in close relationships, some research suggests that this gender difference declines over time. For example, Brown and Auerback (1981) reported that husbands who were in their first years of marriage initiated sex 3 out of 4 times but that husbands in longer term relationships initiated sex only 6 out of 10 times. The same relationship between age and greater equality in sexual initiation, however, was not found by Blumstein and Schwartz (1983), and the opposite results were found by Byers and Heinlein (1989)—younger women reported initiating more sex.

What about sexual initiation in lesbian and gay couples? Blumstein and Schwartz (1983) wrote: "We feel that many lesbians are not comfortable in the role of sexual aggressor and it is a major reason why they have sex less often than other kinds of couples" (p. 214). In gay couples, both partners seem to feel free to initiate sex, which can lead to frequent sex but also to problems such as competition. In both lesbian and gay couples, the more emotionally expressive partner more often initiated sex.

If men are more likely to initiate sex in heterosexual, committed relationships, are women more likely to refuse? Blumstein and Schwartz also asked their couples who was more likely to "refuse to have sex" and found that this factor was more common among women than among men. For example, while 13% of the husbands and 22% of the male cohabitors said they themselves were more likely to refuse sex, 53% of wives and 43% of female cohabitors said they were more likely to. Byers and Heinlein (1989) found that the women in their sample gave more negative responses than men to sexual initiations; however, they also reported a greater number of positive responses. Furthermore, when the researchers controlled for the number of sexual initiations, no significant difference was found in men's and women's responses to sexual initiation.

The studies reviewed above make it clear that sexual initiation in a close relationship is related to gender. Other factors, however, also are related to the likelihood of self-initiation or mutual-initiation of sex in a close relationship. These factors include being the more emotionally expressive partner (Blumstein & Schwartz, 1983) and being sexually satisfied (Blumstein & Schwartz, 1983; Byers & Heinlein, 1989). Blumstein and Schwartz (1983) also identified factors related to the refusal of sex. They reported that the more powerful partner in a couple was more likely to refuse sex and that equality in refusal was positively related to sexual satisfaction, frequency of sex, and overall relationship satisfaction.

How do individuals actually go about initiating and refusing sexual activity? We reported in Chapter 3 that individuals are likely to use indirect strategies (e.g., body movement) to initiate sex and direct strategies (e.g., verbal) to refuse sex (see McCormick, 1979). Research conducted with more committed relationships has found much the same. For example, Brown and Auerback (1981) found, in their study of 50 professional couples, that 60% of the respondents used nonverbal techniques (e.g., kissing, touching, reading sexually explicit material) to initiate sex, while 40% used verbal techniques. The researchers identified five types of verbal initiations: *Let's statements* (e.g., "Let's make love"), *I statements* ("I want to make love to you"), *Comments on the partner's appearance* (e.g., "You look sexy to me"), *Demands* (e.g., "Do it to me"), and *Questions* ("Are you in the mood?"). "Let's" statements and "I" statements were the most common verbal ways of initiating sexual activity. Men were most likely to use "Let's" statements, and women were more likely to use "I" statements.

Sexual Communication and Relationship Satisfaction

Masters and Johnson (1979; Masters, Johnson, & Kolodny, 1986) stated that couples who maintain a high quality of communication about sex are more likely to have a satisfying sexual relationship.

They made this assertion on the basis of their clinical experience. Other research has supported this observation.

With a random sample of 402 married students, Cupach and Comstock (1990) examined the relationship between sexual communication, sexual satisfaction, and overall relationship satisfaction in marriage. Respondents completed the Wheeless, Wheeless, and Baus (1984) Sexual Communication Satisfaction Scale, which consists of 22 items assessing several components, including satisfaction with communication about sexual behavior and willingness to communicate about sex with one's partner. Sexual communication satisfaction was positively correlated with sexual satisfaction (as measured by the Hudson et al. [1981] Sexual Satisfaction Scale) and with overall relationship satisfaction (as measured by Spanier's Dyadic Adjustment Scale). The researchers also found support for a causal model in which sexual communication satisfaction affects overall relationship satisfaction through its effect on the mediating variable of sexual satisfaction. Other research also suggests a positive relationship between sexual communication and either sexual satisfaction or relationship satisfaction (Banmen & Vogel, 1985; Chesney, Blakeney, Cole, & Chan, 1981; Perlman & Abramson, 1982)

Summary

Sex in a close relationship is not isolated or unrelated to behaviors and feelings in the nonsexual areas of the relationship. Having sex in a close relationship can be considered as one behavior among larger groups of behaviors that are important to the close relationship. More specifically, sex may be an act of self-disclosure, intimacy, affection or love, interdependence, maintenance, and exchange. In addition, sexuality (occurrence, frequency, satisfaction) is related to other important dimensions of the relationship—general relationship satisfaction, love, conflict, and equity. These other dimensions both affect and are affected by sexuality in the relationship, and the occurrence, quantity, and quality of sex affects whether the relationship remains intact over time. Effective communication is important to the sexual relationship. Communication can enhance sexual arousal, is necessary for the initiation and refusal of sex, and is related to sexual satisfaction.

6

Sexual Coercion in Developing and Developed Relationships

We had come back from a party and he had drunk too much. . . . At six feet four inches and two hundred pounds he was quite powerful. . . . When we got home I went to bed immediately. He came in, got in bed, and wanted to make love. I wasn't in the mood to do that. He forced himself, by using his strength to pin my arms down. He started kissing me, all the time holding my arms down. . . . I fought him for a long time. I tried to free my arms, but I couldn't. I yelled abuse at him, told him to leave me alone and to stop it. . . . Yes, he had intercourse with me. (a 31-year-old divorced women discussing her former husband, quoted in Russell, 1990, pp. 164-165)

The content of most of this book has been on consensual sexuality and the positive aspects of sexuality for close relationships. The purpose of this chapter is to discuss various forms of sexual coercion in close relationships. The major focus is on women as the victims of sexual coercion in heterosexual relationships, although we acknowledge that, less frequently, men are also victims and that such coercion can occur in homosexual relationships. Instances of sexual coercion in dating situations have filled the mass media in recent years—most notably, the rape trials of William Kennedy Smith and Mike Tyson. As this chapter will show, such incidents, as well

125

as incidents of marital rape such as described above, do not just happen to famous people in the public eye.

This chapter examines several questions: How do we define sexual coercion, and what types of sexual coercion exist in close relationships? How many people are affected by sexual coercion, and how often does it occur? What are people's attitudes and perceptions of date and marital rape? What factors influence the occurrence of sexual coercion in close relationships? What are the effects of sexual coercion in close relationships on both the victim and the relationship?

Sexual Coercion: Definition and Types

Many terms, in addition to *sexual coercion*, are used to refer to behaviors in which one person forces or attempts to force sexual behavior on another. These terms include *sexual assault, sexual aggression, sexual violence, sexual exploitation*, and *rape*. Many researchers use the term *rape*. We, however, believe that the term *sexual coercion* is more inclusive and is associated with fewer assumptions or stereotypes (e.g., *rape* may provoke images of only vaginal-penile penetration). Numerous definitions of *sexual coercion* exist. One example is "the use of physical violence, threats of bodily harm, or psychological, economic, or evaluative pressure to force you, or attempt to force you, into engaging in sexual intercourse, oral sex, or anal sex" (Allgeier, 1986, p. 2).

Several researchers have presented categories or types of sexual coercion in close relationships. We will discuss one typology of marital rape and three typologies that have come from research on sexual coercion in dating relationships. Finkelhor and Yllö (1985) argued, from results of their studies of marital rape, that there are three forms of marital rape, distinguished primarily by the different goals of the spouse. First, *battering rape* is forced sex combined with physical beatings. Second, Finkelhor and Yllö discussed *force-only rape*, in which spouses are not involved in other types of violence or abuse. The husband uses force just in the context of securing sex with his wife. They found that the victims of force-only rapes were more likely to be educated, middle class, and to hold professional jobs than were victims of battering rape. Third, some of the rapes fit into a category called the *obsessive rape*. Husbands involved in this type of rape use force to gain their wives' participation in unusual sexual activities.

The next two typologies emphasize the techniques or strategies used to obtain sexual activity from a dating partner. Muehlenhard and her associates (e.g., Muehlenhard & Cook, 1988; Muehlenhard, Goggins, Jones, & Satterfield, 1991) discussed *violent sexual coercion* or sexual assault by use of physical force or threats of physical force. They also identified *nonviolent sexual coercion*, which includes both verbal sexual coercion (e.g., threatening to terminate the relationship) and sexual coercion that results from "social norms, gender roles, and the relative power of women and men in society" (Muehlenhard et al., 1991, p. 155). Christopher and his associates (Christopher, 1988; Christopher & Frandsen, 1990; Christopher, London, & Owens, 1991) described two types of strategies used to persuade a partner to engage in sexual behavior. *Pressure and manipulation* involves verbal persuasion and persistence and is less forceful than *antisocial acts*, which includes such actions as using or threatening force, expressing anger at the partner, and verbally insulting the partner.

Finally, researchers also have distinguished among types of sexual coercion by *when* such behavior occurs in the dating relationship. For example, Shotland (1989) proposed three types of date rape: *beginning date rape, early date rape*, and *relational date rape*. The distinction between these types is in terms of the length and interpersonal status of the relationship. Shotland's model of date rape will be discussed in more detail later in this chapter.

❧ How Common Is Sexual Coercion in Close Relationships?

Most of the research on rates of sexual coercion in close relationships is survey research with questionnaires or interviews of high school or college samples, although a few studies have had samples of broader populations (e.g., Finkelhor & Yllö, 1985; Kilpatrick et al., 1985; Russell, 1982). The rates of sexual coercion vary by the type of sample (e.g., high school or college women, or women at shelters for battered women) and the particular definition (e.g., physically forced

Table 6.1 Percentage of Women Who Were Victims of Attempted or
Successful Forced Sex by Relationship Type

Relationship	Finkelhor & Yllö (N=326) Percentage of Women	Russell (N=930) Percentage of Women
Acquaintance	3	14
Friend	3	6
Date	10	12
Boyfriend	—	3
Lover/ex-lover	—	6
Husband/ex-husband	10	8

SOURCE: Finkelhor & Yllö, 1985; Russell, 1990

intercourse or coercion of any sexual behavior) and measure of
sexual coercion used (e.g., a scale, a single question, police data).
Most experts believe that incidents of sexual coercion in marital,
dating, and homosexual relationships are underreported for a variety of reasons. These include victims not defining the incident as rape,
fearing revenge from the offender, or feeling concerned that their
story will not be believed by others (e.g., Hart, 1986; Kanin, 1984;
Koss, 1988; Russell, 1990).

Table 6.1 contains summary data from two studies on the percentage of women who reported being victims of forced sex in various
categories of relationships.

Sexual Coercion in Marriage

> I suppose that it could be considered rape. We were married at the
> time and I wanted sex and she didn't, she didn't even want to know.
> I forced her. (a husband cited in Hite, 1981, p. 761)

Several states still have a marital exemption clause in their sexual
assault laws that makes rape within marriage legally impossible. As
of 1990, 8 states still prohibit the prosecution of husbands for rape
of their wives, 26 states have limited marital exemptions (e.g., prosecution is allowed only if the spouses are legally separated or not living
together), and 16 states have no such exemptions (Russell, 1990).
Despite its ambiguous legal status, marital sexual coercion does, in
fact, occur.

Russell (1982, 1990) found that 14% of the married women in her probability sample of almost 1,000 San Francisco women reported behaviors by their husbands that would qualify as sexual assault. In a national survey of married couples (Greeley, 1991), 10% of married women reported being forced to have sex (of this 10%, 25% were assaulted by the spouse, 22% by a friend, 16% by a date or relative, 6% by a stranger, 31% other). Finkelhor and Yllö (1985) found that 10% of married or previously married women in their sample of Boston women (drawn from a larger study of parents) reported being forced by their husbands or cohabiting partners to engage in sex. According to Pagelow (1988), 50% of battered wives are sexually assaulted by their spouses.

Although the statistics cited above are for the *incidence* of sexual coercion (what percentage of people are victimized) in marriage, we also can consider the *frequency* (how often it happens to someone). Russell (1990) found that 31% of the victimized women in a San Francisco sample reported experiencing marital rape once, 37% reported marital rape 2 to 20 times, and 31% reported marital rape more than 20 times. In a Boston sample drawn from family planning centers and women's shelters, 46 women reported forced or attempted forced sex by a spouse (Finkelhor & Yllö, 1985). Of these, 28% reported that the coercion occurred once, 11% said twice, 7% indicated 3 to 10 times, 4% reported a frequency of 11 to 20 times, and 50% said they were sexually assaulted by their spouse more than 20 times.

Sexual Coercion in Dating Relationships

Some of the earliest research on sexual coercion in dating relationships was conducted by Kanin and his colleagues at Purdue University. In one early study, he reported that about 20% of college women indicated someone had attempted to force sexual intercourse on them during a date in the year prior to the survey. About 60% indicated they were the victim of some form of sexual aggression (e.g., forced kissing, petting, oral sex, intercourse) on a date in that time period (Kanin, 1957). It is interesting to note that in a replication study 20 years later at the same university, Kanin and Parcell (1977) found essentially the same rates.

More recent research on victimization indicates that sexual aggression in a dating situation or with a dating partner is still quite common. In samples of high school or college women, 10% to 25% report experiencing forced intercourse. When we look at a broader definition of sexual coercion, 20% to 80% of women report experiencing some form of forced sexual activity (e.g., forced kissing, petting, oral sex, intercourse). The lower percentages are for the more serious behaviors; higher rates are for the less serious activities (e.g., Christopher, 1988; Copenhaver & Grauerholz, 1991; Fenstermaker, 1989; Korman & Leslie, 1982; Koss, Gidycz, & Wisniewski, 1987; Muehlenhard & Linton, 1987; Ward, Chapman, Cohn, White, & Williams, 1991).

Levine and Kanin (1987), in a review of research and theory on this topic, argued that the rates of date and acquaintance (victim and offender know each other in some way) sexual coercion of teenage and college women have been increasing steadily over the last 30 years. They wrote:

> Although this survey of evidence should be viewed with a degree of caution . . . there is nevertheless a preponderance of and a consistency in the evidence from the past 30 years indicating that the college female is increasingly finding herself a target of sexual victimization and violence. This is now also true for female high school seniors (and perhaps even younger teenagers). (p. 145)

Rates of sexual coercion also can be studied from the offender's viewpoint. Surveying men about the degree to which they sexually coerce women, Kanin (1969) found that 25% of the men in his random sample at one college reported at least one sexually aggressive episode (defined as attempting to force intercourse on a woman who responded with offended reactions) in a dating situation since entering college. In addition, 8% of the males from a sample of 32 college campuses reported engaging in behavior that qualifies legally as rape or attempted rape (Koss et al., 1987). Struckman-Johnson (1988), in a survey of college students at one university, reported that 10% of the men admitted they had forced sex on a date. An even greater proportion of men (30% to 40%) said they had used various types of verbal coercion to gain compliance to sexual activity (Craig, Kalichman, & Follingstad, 1989; Koss & Oros, 1982).

Male sexual victimization in dating relationships is studied much less frequently than female victimization. Struckman-Johnson (1988) surveyed 623 students at a large public university. Of the total sample of men ($N = 268$), 16% reported one or more experiences as a victim of forced sex on a heterosexual date during their lifetime. The researcher then received detailed written descriptions of a forced sex incident from 23 male victims. According to the detailed descriptions, most of these men were forced into sex through the use of psychological strategies (e.g., verbal pressure or threats from the woman, expectations of the male role). A few of the men indicated that the women also used some physical coercion.

In another study, Muehlenhard and Cook (1988) gave questionnaires to 507 men in introductory psychology classes. Unwanted kissing, petting, or intercourse was experienced by 93% of these men; unwanted intercourse was experienced by 63% of these men. The most common reasons given by the men for engaging in unwanted intercourse were enticement or seduction (reported by 57% of the male victims), altruism (35%), inexperience (34%), and intoxication (31%).

Sexual Coercion in Homosexual Relationships

Very little research exists on sexual coercion in homosexual relationships. It is difficult to obtain samples of gay men and lesbians, and surveys that focus on forced sex often exclude homosexuals or fail to measure sexual orientation. One exception is a survey study of a small number of gay men ($N = 34$) and lesbian women ($N = 36$) from several colleges (Waterman, Dawson, & Bologna, 1989). Being forced to engage in sexual activity by their most recent partner was reported by 12% of the men and 31% of the women. In addition, 6% of the men and 8% of the women admitted to forcing their most recent partner to engage in sex. In a study of 104 lesbian women, Schilit, Lie, and Montagne (1990) found that 36% of the women said they had experienced physical and/or sexual violence in a lesbian relationship. Unfortunately the authors of this research did not report the data separately for the different types of violence (physical vs. sexual).

In summary, studies assessing the rates of sexual coercion in close relationships show that such activities are not uncommon. A consistent minority of women (about 10% to 25%) report being forced to engage in sexual intercourse by a close partner (date, boyfriend, spouse). As many as 80% of women indicate they have experienced some form of coerced sexual activity (not necessarily intercourse) in a relationship. In addition, anywhere from one-tenth to one-third of college men admit to engaging in sexual coercion in a dating situation. Finally, there is limited evidence that males may be victims of sexual coercion by female partners and that sexual coercion in homosexual relationships also occurs.

ᴥ Attitudes About Sexual Coercion in Close Relationships

Researchers also have investigated people's attitudes and perceptions about sexual coercion, especially of acquaintance or date rape. People's attitudes about sexual coercion in close relationships are important to examine because they can affect behavior and reactions to behaviors of others. Generally this research is of two types. Most involves experimental studies in which subjects are randomly assigned to read or hear hypothetical scenarios of incidents of sexual coercion. Characteristics of the victim, offender, and/or situation are manipulated within the scenarios, and subjects are asked a series of reaction questions about the behavior or the participants. The purpose of these experiments is to determine whether and how these characteristics affect the subjects' perceptions and attitudes about sexual coercion. The second general category of research on attitudes involves survey research in which respondents are asked various questions or given scales to assess their attitudes and perceptions about sexual coercion in close relationships.

Experimental Research on Attitudes About Sexual Coercion

In the experiments, the independent variables include type of sexually coercive behavior, relationship between the victim and offender, sex of the victim or offender, physical attractiveness of the victim or offender, level of the victim's suggestive behavior and/or resistance, and aspects of the situation (e.g., where the date took place, who paid for the date). Much of this research also has examined whether male subjects and female subjects react in the same way to the vignettes.

Dependent variables in these experiments generally include perceptions about whether the incident was sexual coercion or how acceptable or justifiable the behavior was, attributions about responsibility or intent for the act, attributions of positive or negative emotions to the individuals, and other views about the victim and the offender.

The vignette in Box 6.1, is an example of what might be used in this type of research. Words in italics are possible independent variables that would vary, depending on which version of the scenario the subject received. Imagine that you were asked to read this scenario.

BOX 6.1

Example Material in an Experimental Study

Sally and John met in their English composition class. They have been *dating casually* (or seriously) for several weeks. Last Saturday night they went on a date. John took Sally to a very expensive restaurant for dinner, wine, and conversation. *John paid for all of the expenses* (or they split the expenses) of the date. After dinner, they returned to Sally's apartment for another bottle of wine. Both Sally and John were *slightly intoxicated* (or very intoxicated). John told Sally that he wanted to have sexual intercourse with her. She replied that she was not ready to do so at this point in their relationship. John then used *his greater physical size and strength* (or verbal persuasion

and pressure) to force Sally to have sexual intercourse with him. She told him to stop and tried to get away, but she was not successful.

After reading such a scenario in an experiment, you might be asked a series of questions such as:

1. How responsible was Sally for the incident in the scenario?
2. Should John's behavior be reported to the police?
3. To what extent does the behavior in the story constitute rape?

You would most likely be asked to respond to these questions on a scale such as:

Definitely   Definitely
is rape   not rape

The major results of these experiments can be summarized in three categories, including the results from independent variables about *the situation or act*, independent variables about *victim or offender characteristics*, and independent variables about the *subjects* in the experiment.

Factors Related to the Situation or Act

1. More coercive acts (e.g., physical force compared to verbal pressure) are associated with more negative and fewer positive feelings directed toward the offender and less acceptance of the act (Fenstermaker, 1989; Garcia, Milano, & Quijano, 1989; Struckman-Johnson & Struckman-Johnson, 1991).

2. The more ambiguous the incident about whether or not it is rape (e.g., it is unclear to what extent the victim wants intercourse), the more lenient and less punishing subjects are toward the offender, the more justifiable they see the act, and the less favorable they are toward the victim (Johnson & Jackson, 1988; Muehlenhard, Linton, Felts, & Andrews, 1985).

3. Low levels of force and late onset of victim protests contribute to more blaming of the victim, while more force and more and earlier victim protests result in a greater likelihood of viewing the offender as violent and the act as rape (Shotland & Goodstein, 1983).

4. Location (e.g., car, apartment) and activity (e.g., movie, dinner) of the date affect ratings of responsibility (Fenstermaker, 1989). For example, going to the man's apartment increases the responsibility ratings of the woman.

5. When the woman asks the man out or the man pays all of the date expenses, rape is seen as more justifiable (Muehlenhard, 1988; Muehlenhard, Friedman, & Thomas, 1985).

Factors Related to the Victim or Offender

The relationship of the victim and offender, in combination with other factors, affects beliefs about responsibility and causes of the incident (Bridges, 1991; Bridges & McGrail, 1989; Fenstermaker, 1989; Gerdes, Dammann, & Heilig, 1988). For example, the closer the relationship between the victim and the offender, the less likely the incident is viewed as sexual coercion.

Factors Related to Subject Characteristics

1. Male subjects compared to female subjects tend to be more lenient toward the offender, less favorable toward the victim, and more accepting of the act (Bridges, 1991; Bridges & McGrail, 1989; Johnson & Jackson, 1988; Struckman-Johnson & Struckman-Johnson, 1991).
2. Subjects holding more traditional attitudes toward women see date rape as more justifiable (Muehlenhard, 1988; Muehlenhard, Linton, Felts, & Andrews, 1985) or are less likely to see the act as rape (Fischer, 1986).
3. Women who believe that "leading a man on" justifies rape judge victims more negatively and as more responsible and are less likely to see the incident as rape, especially if the victim's behavior was suggestive (Muehlenhard & MacNaughton, 1988).

Survey Research on Attitudes
About Sexual Coercion

As mentioned earlier, the second set of research on attitudes and perceptions about sexual coercion in close relationships is survey research, usually self-administered questionnaires. Most survey research, however, focuses on involvement in sexual coercion (see the section above on rates of sexual coercion in close relationships) or on the relationship between certain attitudes and involvement (see the section below on factors associated with sexual coercion). Therefore only a few additional studies will be mentioned briefly here.

In a survey of junior high school students (Lewis, 1988), rape among married couples was viewed as acceptable by 87% of the boys and 79% of the girls. Sixty-five percent of the boys and 45% of the girls felt that after dating a woman for 6 months or more, it is acceptable for a man to force sex on the woman. In a survey of high school students, Giarrusso, Johnson, Goodchilds, and Zellman (1979) found that 12% of the girls and 39% of the boys thought it was acceptable for a boy to force sex on a girl if he had spent a lot of money on the girl. Finally, Sweet (1985) reported that 51% of men and 42% of women in a study of college students thought it was acceptable for a man to use force to obtain sex if "she gets him excited."

In a review of research on young people's attitudes toward date and acquaintance rape, White and Humphrey (1991) concluded that "the consensus among American students from junior high school through college is that forced sexual intercourse on a date rarely constitutes rape" (p. 45). They also stated that this attitude is stronger for men than for women.

We can see from the experimental and survey research on attitudes toward sexual coercion in close relationships that many factors affect people's perceptions of the justifiability of the act, attribution of intent or responsibility, and judgments of the people involved. These factors include gender of the respondent, respondent attitudes toward women, nature of the victim-offender relationship, ambiguity of the situation, and victim's behavior. In addition, high school and college students often do not define sexual coercion in close relationships as inappropriate. Finally, males tend to be somewhat more tolerant of such coercion than are women.

❧ Factors Related to the Occurrence of Sexual Coercion in Close Relationships

Research and analysis of sexual coercion in close relationships have led to the discovery of numerous factors associated with this behavior. These contributing factors occur at different levels of analysis, including individual level factors, relationship level factors, group level factors, and cultural (or societal) level factors. In this section we briefly discuss these correlates of sexual coercion in close relationships.

Behaviors and Characteristics of the Individuals

Victim and Offender Behaviors

Numerous researchers have noted that one behavior—drug or alcohol use by the victim, the offender, or both—occurs in the majority of incidents of sexual assault in close relationships (e.g., Copenhaver & Grauerholz, 1991; Frieze, 1983; Harney & Muehlenhard, 1991; Kanin, 1984; Koss, 1988; Lundberg-Love & Geffner, 1989; Miller & Marshall, 1987; Russell, 1984). In addition, use of alcohol may be a strategy used in combination with other tactics to influence the partner to have sex (Christopher & Frandsen, 1990). Alcohol use may lessen one's inhibitions against deviant or nonconforming behavior and is often a part of dating situations and dating expectations (e.g., a party).

Other verbal or nonverbal behaviors of the victim (such as wearing certain clothing) have been discussed as factors affecting sexual coercion (e.g., Grauerholz & Solomon, 1989; Harney & Muehlenhard, 1991; Kanin & Parcell, 1977; Shotland & Goodstein, 1983). For example, 65% of the women in one study (Miller & Marshall, 1987) reported they had engaged in sexual teasing although they did not want to have sexual intercourse. Muehlenhard and Hollabaugh (1988) argued that women sometimes offer token resistance to sexual activity usually as a result of the pressures of the sexual double standard. Such token resistance may lead to miscommunication and different expectations about sexual activity in the relationship.

Victim and Offender Characteristics

Characteristics of the victim and the offender also have been researched. We discuss first some demographic characteristics and then attitudes of the individuals involved in sexual coercion. In the study by Frieze (1983) of marital rape, women who were less educated, who had never been employed, and who had more children were more likely to be assaulted by their spouses. These women were seen as having less power than their husbands in the marital relationship, putting them at greater risk than other women for victimization and making it less likely that they could leave the marriage to avoid victimization.

Kanin (1969) compared the demographic similarity (how similar the male and female partners were on age, religion, status, and perceived intelligence) between sexually aggressive and nonaggressive couples. He found significantly less similarity between the members of couples involved in sexual violence than between those not involved.

Furthermore, aspects of one's family background are associated with sexual coercion in close relationships. Coming from a violent family of origin (Frieze, 1983; Grauerholz & Solomon, 1989; Muehlenhard et al., 1991; Russell, 1984) and prior involvement in sexual abuse or rape have been related to a higher rate of current experience with sexual coercion (Frieze, 1983; Lundberg-Love & Geffner, 1989). This type of background and prior involvement may put one at greater risk for current involvement in sexual coercion for at least two reasons. First, victims may inadvertently seek out close relationship partners with characteristics similar to those of their past abusers. Second, offenders may be taught through socialization the justifications, excuses, and techniques of sexual coercion.

In addition, for both victims and offenders, more traditional sex roles, traditional attitudes toward women, and traditional masculine traits (especially for men) are associated with greater involvement in sexual coercion in dating situations or within close relationships (e.g., Kanin & Parcell, 1977; Lundberg-Love & Geffner, 1989; Muehlenhard & Falcon, 1990; Poppen & Segal, 1988; Russell, 1982; Warshaw & Parrot, 1991). Russell (1990), however, reported that this association was not the case for the wives in her study; that is, women raped by their husbands were no more traditional than other wives. Interestingly, women who hold feminist views and/or who share in the expenses of the date have been found to be at greater risk of such victimization, perhaps because they threaten men's sense of masculinity or put themselves in situations of greater risk (Korman & Leslie, 1982).

Other attitudes and beliefs held by individuals have been found to be related to involvement in sexual coercion in close relationships. For example, Muehlenhard et al. (1991) discussed several beliefs about close relationships that contribute to sexual coercion. These include the beliefs that "close relationships should be private and sexual" and "the male should be in control." These beliefs support sexual violence because sex in close relationships is seen as obligatory, as male dominated, and as private (others outside the relationship have no right to intervene). Similarly Harney and Muehlenhard (1991) discussed the effects that dating scripts (e.g., traditional scripts in which the men are to initiate dates and sex and the women are to be passive recipients; that is men pay for dates, and women exchange sex in return) can have on such coercive behavior. Essentially these beliefs and scripts set up roles and situations in close relationships for women and men to follow that encourage or reward men for sexual achievement and powerful, controlling behavior, and women for submissive, passive, and victimlike behavior.

The acceptance of rape myths—adversarial sexual beliefs or attitudes accepting the use of force to obtain sex—also is associated with sexual coercion experience (Burt, 1991; Christopher, London,

& Owens, 1991; Craig et al., 1989; Lundberg-Love & Geffner, 1989; Muehlenhard & Cook, 1988).

Characteristics of the Relationship

Several relationship level or couple factors have been related to involvement in sexual coercion; that is, some relationships, because of the interaction patterns of the couple and the context of the relationship, have a greater chance of involving sexual coercion.

Miscommunication, either verbal or nonverbal, about sexual expectations, desires, or activities for the relationship has been discussed by many researchers as playing a major role in sexual coercion in intimate relationships (e.g., Abbey, 1991; Grauerholz & Solomon, 1989; Kanin, 1969, 1984; Lundberg-Love & Geffner, 1989; Muehlenhard, 1988; Muehlenhard & Linton, 1987). Related to such miscommunication are the findings that men and women often hold different views and expectations about the courtship process (Lloyd, 1991) and that men and women have different perceptions or make different attributions about another's sexual interest or intent (Abbey, 1982; Abbey et al., 1987; Shotland, 1989; Shotland & Craig, 1988). Some of these issues were discussed in earlier chapters. Such conflicting perceptions and expectations may lead to violence as the male either incorrectly assumes that the female wants sex and/or uses force to ensure that his expectations are met.

Researchers also have pointed to aspects of the relationship as influencing the experience of sexual coercion. For instance, Lloyd (1991) stressed the patriarchal (male dominant) aspect of intimate relationships, as well as the role that romanticism (e.g., the male should sweep the female off her feet, and the female should comply) may play in sexual coercion.

Christopher, London, and Owens (1991) have shown that the levels of conflict and ambivalence in the relationship are positively related to the use of pressure/manipulation and antisocial strategies of sexual coercion in intimate relationships. Marital rape has been associated with other forms of violence or battering in the marriage (e.g., Frieze, 1983; Russell, 1982) and with relationships involving lower quality and more disagreement (Bowker, 1983). Hence sexual violence in close relationships may for some relationships be merely a symptom of a relationship that is filled with conflict and violence in general.

Finally, most of the research on the effects of length or stage of relationship on sexual coercion in dating relationships has found that sexual coercion is most likely to occur in relationships that are in early (e.g., casual), but not beginning (e.g., first date), stages. For example, Copenhaver and Grauerholz (1991) found that such violence was more likely after about 1 month of dating than it was for the first or second date. Other researchers have found that most sexual coercion occurs in casual pairings (Kanin & Parcell, 1977) or in occasional date pairings (Kanin, 1969, 1984). Yet Craig et al. (1989) found that men involved in first or second date relationships were more accepting of the use of force to obtain sex than were men in steady date relationships.

Membership in Certain Groups

> University of Florida: Six Pi Lambda Phi fraternity members are accused of raping a 17-year-old female freshman student who had been at the fraternity house for a rush party for the group's "little sister" program. (Little sisters are females affiliated with, but not members of, the fraternity.) (from Warshaw, 1988, p. 104)

Group level factors have focused on the influence of peer groups, including fraternities, on sexual coercion in close relationships. Numerous researchers during the last several decades have shown that male peer groups may support sexual coercion by socializing men to accept aggression as an acceptable way to obtain sex (e.g., Copenhaver & Grauerholz, 1991; Kanin, 1957; Kanin & Parcell, 1977; Lloyd, 1991; Martin & Hummer, 1989). In addition, peer group use of alcohol is common, and, as already discussed, the use of alcohol is associated with sexual coercion.

In a study of 71 self-identified date rapists, Kanin (1984) reported that, compared with a control group of men who had not raped, these men were part of a "highly erotic-oriented peer group socialization which started during the junior high and high school years" (p. 98). He argued that these individuals have a broader range of acceptability in terms of how many sexual partners they desire and what strategies they are willing to use to gain their sexual goals.

Several studies have focused on fraternity men or on sorority women. For example, a recent study of sexual coercion among college students (Copenhaver & Grauerholz, 1991) assessed the role of sororities in sexual assault in close relationships. These authors surveyed a random sample of sorority women at a Midwestern university. About 13% of the women reported sexual coercion while in college that would meet the legal definition of rape. In over 90% of the cases, the woman knew her attacker. Responses indicated that almost 60% of the reported incidents of sexual coercion occurred at a fraternity house or involved a fraternity member. Alcohol was associated with 96% of these incidents. The authors argued that being active in a sorority increases one's risk of sexual coercion.

In a study comparing a group of fraternity men with a group of independents (Boeringer, Shehan, & Akers, 1991), it was found that the fraternity men, to a greater degree than independents, had associations with men who engaged in coercive sex, were likely to receive reinforcement from friends for sexually coercive activities, were likely to participate in nonphysical sexual coercion, and were likely to use drugs and alcohol as a tactic for obtaining sexual goals.

Characteristics of Our Culture

Griffiths (1971) coined the phrase "Rape, the all-American crime," meaning that certain characteristics of American culture support, accept, and perpetuate sexual coercion, including that found in close relationships. She saw rape as a tolerated part of our everyday life. In a sense it is normative behavior in certain situations.

What aspects of our culture contribute to sexual coercion? Traditional socialization about *gender roles* and sexuality (e.g., Muehlenhard et al., 1991; Russell, 1984), *power inequality* between men and women (e.g., Frieze, 1983; Grauerholz & Solomon, 1989; Kanin, 1969; Lloyd, 1991), and the role of social institutions such as the *mass media* (Harney & Muehlenhard, 1991; Muehlenhard et al., 1991) have been the factors most often discussed at the cultural or societal level as contributing to sexual coercion in close relationships. Although these factors may seem far removed from a particular incident of sexual coercion in a close relationship, as we have discussed elsewhere in this chapter, they are not. These cultural factors influence what men and women believe about sexuality, courtship, and appropriate gender roles. Such beliefs, in turn, affect male-female sexual interactions, including those that involve sexual coercion.

What can be concluded from this discussion of individual, relationship, group, and cultural factors contributing to sexual coercion in intimate relationships? One way to summarize these factors is by placing them in models of sexual coercion in close relationships.

⍣ A Model of Sexual Coercion in Dating Relationships

Models of sexual coercion in dating relationships are attempts to organize, rank, and make sense of the various causal factors that research has shown to affect sexual coercion. Shotland's (1989) model of date rape acknowledges at least three different types of date rape (beginning, early, relational) and focuses on the couple as the unit of analysis; that is, date rape is seen not from the point of view of individual victims or offenders but as a couple event. Shotland emphasized factors of miscommunication, gender differences in the threshold for judging sexual intent, poor impulse control, need for more sexual activity, sense of the relationship as inequitable, a romantic script, and rape supportive attitudes. Which factors are most important, however, varies somewhat by the type of date rape.

Shotland argued that in *beginning date rape,* which happens during the first few dates, the rapist simply may use the date situation to engage in a rape that is less likely to be defined by others as rape. These men may have a greater need for sexual interaction and diversity than other men, may be somewhat antisocial, and are probably recidivists or repeat offenders who have raped more than one partner during beginning dating. Women increase their risk of rape by such men by dating large numbers of men. Poor communication does not play a major role in beginning date rape because the man and the woman probably are aware that intercourse is not yet appropriate, especially from the woman's point of view.

In contrast to beginning date rape, Shotland (1989) posited that *early date rape,* which occurs after several dates, can be explained primarily in terms of "normal courtship processes that affect men and women of college age" (p. 252). Especially critical are the gender differences in expectations and perceptions of dating and sexuality and in the relationship between love and sex, and the miscommunication that results from these gender differences. We discussed previously how such miscommunication can contribute to sexual coercion. Other courtship processes involved in early date rape (also discussed previously) include concern with playing traditional gender roles (males initiate sex and females regulate it) and the perpetuation of a double standard. In addition, various attitudes and characteristics of sexually aggressive males (e.g., belief in rape myths, acceptance of interpersonal violence, high need for sexual activity) contribute to the risk of sexual coercion in the early dating stage.

Finally, in *relational date rape*, the man's perception of power inequity (with the woman having greater power) is one factor contributing to sexual coercion. The man also might feel that he has invested enough (time, energy, money, affection) to have earned sexual intercourse at this point in the relationship, and he may resent the woman's resistance to it. Comparing the couple's lack of sexual activity to that of other couples and the knowledge that the female partner has had prior sexual experience also can increase the likelihood of sexual coercion in the relational stage. Furthermore, a couple's somewhat conservative but also ambiguous sexual standards, common among couples who have dated awhile and still have not had intercourse, may result in confusion, anger, or frustration that contributes to sexual aggression. Miscommunication, Shotland argued, is unlikely to be the major cause of this type of rape because, by this time, members of a couple are familiar with each other's sexual attitudes and standards.

For recent discussions of other models of sexual aggression against women, including sexual aggression in close relationships, see Christopher, Owens, and Stecker (1991), Lundberg-Love and Geffner (1989), and Malamuth, Sockloskie, Koss, and Tanaka (1991).

Outcomes of Sexual Coercion
in Close Relationships

In this section we discuss some of the limited research on the outcomes of sexual coercion in close relationships. Most of the research on outcomes or consequences of sexual coercion has focused on the outcomes of rape, in general, or of stranger rape. In addition, most research has focused on the emotional outcomes for the victim. We review the research that does exist on the individual and relationship level outcomes of sexual coercion in marriage and dating relationships.

Outcomes for the Victim

Research on the reactions of victims to marital, date, and acquaintance sexual assault indicates similar findings. Depression, anxiety, distrust, anger, fear, and guilt are all common reactions (Finkelhor & Yllö, 1985; Gidycz & Koss, 1991; King & Webb, 1981; Kirkpatrick & Kanin, 1957; Koss, Dinero, Seibel, & Cox, 1988; Muehlenhard et al., 1991; Murnen, Perot, & Byrne, 1989). Murnen et al. (1989) reported that women experience more guilt in response to sexual coercion involving verbal coercion than physical coercion. Women may feel that when only verbal coercion was used, they should have been able to resist the assault. In addition, Koss et al. (1988) pointed out that long-term depression is especially likely for women who continue to have contact with the offender. Finally, many women report physical injuries (e.g., bruises, cuts) and physical reactions (e.g., nausea). Negative reactions were not limited to the short term. Victims reported negative reactions decades after the assault, including fear, inability to trust, and apprehension about men (Finkelhor & Yllö, 1985).

Outcomes for the Relationship

In their study of marital rape, Finkelhor and Yllö (1985) found that women reported several consequences of sexual coercion for their relationships. More specifically, women felt divided between leaving the relationship or staying and having to deny the assault and to deal with their anger. Wanting to leave or actually leaving the marriage also was reported by many of the women in Frieze's study (1983). On the basis of a national survey, Greeley (1991) reported that being a victim of sexual coercion is negatively correlated with marital happiness.

Women also reported a decrease in sexual satisfaction and an increase in sexual dysfunctions and in difficulties with sexual activities similar to those that occurred in the assault. One woman in the study by Finkelhor and Yllö (1985) said, "Until this day, I hate sex. I don't get nothing out of it. I hate it so bad. It seems like every time I have it, it's just a flashback" (p. 129). Some women had to cope with an unintended pregnancy or abortion as a result of the assault. These consequences for the sexual aspects of relationships also have been reported by victims of date and acquaintance rape (Gidycz & Koss, 1991; Koss et al., 1988).

One of the most common relational outcomes of sexual coercion in a close relationship is distrust of the partner and, sometimes, of other relationships, especially with men (Finkelhor & Yllö, 1985; Gidycz & Koss, 1991; King & Webb, 1981; Koss et al., 1988). In fact, most researchers argue that the closer the relationship in which the coercion occurs, the greater the level of distrust that develops (King & Webb, 1981; Koss et al., 1988).

One victim of marital rape explained her feelings this way:

> My whole body was being abused. I feel if I'd been raped by a stranger, I could have dealt with it a whole lot better. . . . When a stranger does it, he doesn't know me, I don't know him. He's not doing it to me as a person, personally. With your husband, it becomes personal. You say, this man knows me. He knows my feelings. He knows me intimately, and then to do this to me—it's such personal abuse. (Finkelhor & Yllö, 1985, p. 118)

Another stated:

> I've had a very hard time trusting men. . . . I can't say I hate guys. I have the right reasons to, I know. I think Jimmy ruined it, so that it is going to take a long time before I can hold down a relationship with a guy." (p. 128)

It is clear from this brief review of outcomes of sexual coercion in close relationships that victims experience a wide range of negative emotional and physical consequences, both on a short-term basis and over time. These effects occur in both dating and marital situations. They also are likely to occur in homosexual relationships, although there is little research on this. In addition, there are negative outcomes for the relationship and other relationships, including distrust of men and sexual problems.

❧ Summary

In this chapter we discussed some of the literature on sexual coercion in close relationships. The major focus was on date and marital sexual assault. Topics included categories or types of coercion, rates of sexual coercion in close relationships, people's perceptions of these incidents and those involved in them, factors that influence such behavior, a causal model of sexual coercion in dating relationships, and the consequences of sexual coercion for the victim and the relationship.

The research reviewed demonstrates several types of sexual coercion in close relationships. Sexual coercion affects many people and is influenced by a wide range of individual, relationship, group, and societal level factors. These factors include feelings of hostility, alcohol use, peer support, miscommunication, relationship scripts, male-female socialization, and power imbalances between men and women. The outcomes of sexual coercion in close relationships involve short- and long-term negative emotions, physical trauma, and relationship difficulties.

7

Epilogue

❧ Summary of the Book

The focus of this book has been on sexual expression in close relationships. We discussed sexual attitudes, behaviors, satisfaction, desires, and motivations in the context of close heterosexual and homosexual relationships (dating, cohabiting, and marital). We also discussed how these sexual aspects are related to other characteristics of the relationship. We emphasized mostly current research (covering the last two decades) from the United States and other Western nations.

In our first chapter we presented an overview of sexual attitudes about close relationships, including some historical and cross-cultural data. Most people today, especially young adults, believe that sex in dating relationships is acceptable within a loving relationship. Abstinence and the traditional double standard have declined over time, while conditional double standards and permissiveness with and without affection have become more common. Research also shows that most American adults do not approve of extramarital sexual relationships.

In Chapter 2 we focused on the beginning or initiation of a sexual relationship. We discussed how two people get together and the factors that affect the likelihood they will become attracted to each other. The role of sexuality in the attraction process was discussed in two ways. We examined whether the predictors of sexual attraction are the same as the predictors of romantic attraction (physical attractiveness is a more important predictor of sexual attraction). We summarized research findings on how a potential partner's sexual past affects the attraction process.

How sex is initiated and negotiated in the developing relationship was the topic of Chapter 3. Among the conclusions from this chapter were that sexual interaction in close relationships is more scripted than it is spontaneous and that both men and women are involved in initiating a sexual interaction. Furthermore, the path to sexual intimacy can include miscommunication, misperceptions, and misunderstandings. Finally, we discussed the increasing importance of disclosure about past sexual experiences and communication about condom use prior to an initial sexual contact because of the threat of the AIDS virus.

In Chapter 4 we focused on sexual behaviors and sexual satisfaction in close relationships. We summarized the diversity in sexual behaviors, including in prevalence and frequency. Also discussed was how the frequency of sexual activity declines both over the course of a relationship and over one's lifetime. Finally, we presented research showing that the best predictors of sexual satisfaction are frequent sex and (for women) experiencing orgasms.

The relationship between sexual and other characteristics of a close relationship was summarized in Chapter 5. We discussed how sex has several functions (e.g., self-disclosure, intimacy, a maintenance strategy) within a close relationship. Research also was presented that shows how sexual frequency is related to relationship satisfaction, love, conflict, and equity. In addition, we discussed the ways that sexuality can affect whether the partners of a close relationship stay together. The importance of communication for sexuality in the close relationship also was noted.

In Chapter 6, literature on sexual coercion in close relationships was reviewed. Several conclusions emerged from this final chapter. First, sexual coercion in dating and marital relationships is not atypical and affects many couples. Furthermore, such coercion is, to a substantial degree, the result of characteristics of our culture (e.g., gender inequality) and of the context (situation, scripts, roles) of dating and courtship. Finally, sexual coercion in close relationships has many negative outcomes for both the victim and the relationship.

♨ A Major Theme

Across the chapters of this volume, one theme that emerged was the many gender differences in sexuality in close relationships. Generally men are more permissive toward and interested in sexuality than women. For example, men hold more permissive sexual standards for all types of relationships than women, initiate sexual interaction (at all periods in the relationship) more often than women, rate physical pleasure as a more important reason to engage in sex than do women, and are more likely than women to engage in extramarital sex. Men are more likely than women to assume that others are sexually interested (to misinterpret sexual interest or intent). Finally, men are more tolerant of and less likely to be victimized by sexual coercion than are women.

There are several explanations for such gender differences in sexuality in close relationships. The differential socialization of men and women in our society, including the transmission of traditional sex roles, contributes to these differences; that is, we teach men to have and then reward them for their greater permissiveness and interest in sex. Similarly we raise women to be more conservative and cautious in their sexuality. Related to this explanation is that men and women acquire different sexual scripts for their own gender, with the script for male "actors" containing more permissive "roles" and "lines" than the script for female "actors." Sociobiologists, on the other hand, would emphasize the reproductive imperatives that guide men to be more permissive and sexually active to ensure that they father many children, while women must be careful in their selection of and activity with sexual partners to ensure the survival of their limited offspring.

❧ Methodological Issues

In the process of writing on sexuality in close relationships, we began to think about several methodological issues. We summarize these concerns here because they deal with weaknesses and gaps in the empirical literature that need to be addressed in the future.

The first concern is that much of the research uses either questionnaires or paper-and-pencil experiments (in which subjects read and react to limited information about a target person). Of course, these methods provide us with important types of data on sexuality in close relationships (e.g., data from large samples and on causal relationships, respectively). Also the often private and controversial nature of the topic—sexuality in close relationships—contributes to the use of these methods relative to others. These methods, however, have limitations. The questionnaire research may suffer from self-report biases (under- or overreporting) and memory problems, and the experiments are hindered by artificiality. For example, sexual coercion in dating and marital relationships probably is underreported, yet other forms of behavior, such as frequency of intercourse, might be overreported in questionnaire studies. In addition, having experimental subjects give initial perceptions of hypothetical couples based on limited information to assess sexual standards or perceptions of sexual coercion is not a task closely related to real-world interactions.

The second concern is that we need to develop further other research strategies to gain access to different types of data and to improve the reliability and validity of our research results. We suggest that at least three alternative methods be used more often. First, research in this area might include more unstructured *interview studies* of couples about the sexual aspects of their relationships to obtain more detailed and descriptive data. Second, additional field or *observational studies* of couples negotiating various aspects of sexual interaction and communicating about sexuality would increase the external validity (reality) and processual nature of the data (information about what variables affect what over time). Such studies would have to be in public settings, such as bars, or in private settings using observers or audio-video equipment (with informed consent). Finally, we recommend the use of *diaries or logs* that would be kept over time by couples and would contain information about sexual expression in their relationships. Logs or diaries could help improve self-report data in terms of memory biases and obtain data on sexuality in close relationships as a process occurring over time.

The third concern is that too much of the research on sexuality in close relationships uses the individual as the *unit of analysis;* that is, researchers obtain the data from individuals about sexuality, but the information is abstracted from their real relationships. Even when data are obtained from both members of the couple, it often is analyzed at the individual level. Because of the topic—sexuality in close relationships—the unit of analysis should more often be the couple. For example, if estimates on how often the couple has intercourse are obtained from both members of the couple, a researcher might create a couple score on this variable (using the average of the two estimates). Or researchers might have couples provide joint accounts of sexual interactions.

Related to both of the problems discussed above is the fourth concern, that we conduct more *longitudinal panel studies* of couples. These are studies in which the same couples are followed over time. The couples may be observed, fill out questionnaires, or participate in interviews at two or more points in time. Only a few such studies exist (e.g., Blumstein & Schwartz, 1983; Peplau et al., 1977; Udry, 1980), partly due to their costly and time-consuming nature. Despite these limitations, panel studies are important because they allow researchers to study particular relationships over time and to look at topics such as what factors will affect the timing of first intercourse, how sexuality changes over the course of a relationship, and what sexual aspects of the relationship will contribute to an increase in commitment or the likelihood that the couple will stay together. In addition, we can separate out the effects of factors such as maturation or aging, length of a relationship, and stage of a relationship, which cannot be distinguished in cross-sectional studies (those that look at couples or individuals at one point in time).

The fifth concern is that research on sexuality in close relationships too often includes only college students, uses nonprobability samples (not random or not representative), and/or uses small samples. Exceptions to the focus on college students include, for example, Hunt (1974), DeLamater and MacCorquodale (1979), and Blumstein and Schwartz (1983). Furthermore, most of these samples contain predominately white, middle-class, heterosexual volunteers. (Blumstein and Schwartz, 1983, is a notable exception.) This predominance means, of course, that we must be wary in *generalizing the results* of the research to all college students, noncollege students, younger or older adults, nonwhites, and gays or lesbians. More studies are needed that attempt to study sexual expression in close relationships in these other populations.

Such studies, of course, require adequate funding of large grants by the government. On occasion, the administration or Congress attempts to legislate policies that would prohibit government financial support of large-scale research surveys, especially on sexuality. We see these attempts as a distressing trend that could seriously limit efforts to obtain reliable and valid sexuality information that is needed to deal with social problems such as sexual assault, sexual dysfunctions, sexually transmitted diseases, unwanted pregnancies, and abortions.

The sixth concern is that the limited *cross-cultural research* that exists has shown the need to be cautious when transferring a conceptual or operational (e.g., a scale) definition of a concept from one society to another. For example, the meaning of *sexual permissiveness* may vary by culture such that scales and definitions used in the United States cannot simply be translated and used elsewhere. See Clement (1990) for a more detailed discussion of this point. In addition, we need more cross-cultural research on all aspects of sexuality in close relationships. For a more detailed discussion of research on sexuality in close relationships, see Orbuch and Harvey (1991).

๖ Areas for Future Research

We would like to note *gaps in knowledge* in the existing literature and, hence, where future research should focus. In addition to the areas discussed above, researchers should look more often at the sexual victimization of homosexuals (gays and lesbians) and male heterosexuals in close relationships. We need additional research on how AIDS can affect the future of a close relationship. Studies that focus on postmarital and cohabiting sexual expression and sexuality in cross-sex friendships (not just on premarital and marital relationships) would add to the knowledge base. In addition, although there is a fair amount of research on sexual satisfaction, there is much less on sexual desire, sexual interest, and other subjective assessments concerning sexuality in a relationship. We also would like to see more research that attempts to assess the meaning of sexuality to couples in their close relationships and how couples negotiate situations in which partners hold different perceptions or meanings for sexual activity.

Further theoretical development would benefit all research efforts in this field. Several of the areas reviewed in this book were atheoretical. In other words, more research needs to be theory-driven, and we need to accumulate and integrate research findings across areas in order to build theories and models. As one example, we believe that *script theory* (Gagnon, 1990), with its emphasis on sexual scripts at the cultural level and sexual scripts idiosyncratic to the couple or to the relationship, has a great deal to offer the field of sexuality in close relationships.

‎ Thoughts on Application

We conclude with a brief discussion of three issues related to the application of research on sexuality in close relationships. We feel that more work needs to be done to share the empirical results of such research with the public, therapists, and the media.

Recently Schwartz (1992) discussed the failure of most relationship researchers to disseminate their findings to the general public via the mass media. She pointed out some of the barriers to doing so (e.g., lack of time, fear of being misunderstood). Yet she made a good argument for why we should make this effort, including that the "demand for reliable information is there. The public has an appetite for research findings—particularly on relationships. . . . And if they can't get the real thing . . . they will rely on what's available" (p. 1). Schwartz went on to argue that three changes will be necessary to increase the involvement of researchers with the media and the public: a change in values so that such activities are seen as credible and acceptable, a change in rewards so that these activities count for something in university tenure and promotion decisions, and a change in training so that researchers know how best to present themselves and their findings.

Next, it seems to us that much of the research on sexuality in close relationships contains findings that could be useful to therapists working in relationship, marital, and sexual therapy. It is important, therefore, to develop strategies for sharing our findings with such professionals. For example, researchers could give workshops to groups of local therapists, present papers at professional meetings of therapists, and occasionally publish in applied and clinical journals read by therapists. Such interaction with clinicians would benefit researchers as well, for clinicians' conceptions of sexuality in close relationships, based in the real experiences of their clients, could provide many ideas for our empirical and theoretical work.

A final issue of application deals with the relationship between scientific knowledge and people's behavior. Several writers have discussed the notion of a feedback loop between scientific research on sexuality and people's sexual behavior (Byrne, 1977; Gagnon, 1975; Gergen, 1973; Hendrick & Hendrick, 1992; Robinson, 1976); that is, it has been suggested that the scientific findings on sexuality in close relationships (sometimes reported in the mass media) influence people's sexual behavior in close relationships. In turn, sexual behavior then becomes the data we study once again. We believe that this feedback loop itself is worthy of empirical research. To what extent and in what ways does scientific knowledge influence people's sexual behavior? How does that behavior then affect our research emphases in the area of sexuality and close relationships?

References

Abbey, A. (1982). Sex differences in attributions for friendly behaviors: Do males misperceive females' friendliness? *Journal of Personality and Social Psychology, 42,* 830-838.

Abbey, A. (1987). Misperceptions of friendly behavior as sexual interest: A survey of naturally occurring incidents. *Psychology of Women Quarterly, 11,* 173-194.

Abbey, A. (1991). Misperceptions as an antecedent of acquaintance rape: A consequence of ambiguity in communication between men and women. In A. Parrot & L. Bechhofer (Eds.), *Acquaintance rape: The hidden crime* (pp. 96-111). New York: John Wiley.

Abbey, A., Cozzarelli, C., McLaughlin, K., & Harnish, R. J. (1987). The effects of clothing and dyad sex composition on perceptions of sexual intent: Do women and men evaluate these cues differently? *Journal of Applied Social Psychology, 17,* 108-126.

Abbey, A., & Melby, C. (1986). The effects of nonverbal cues on gender differences in perceptions of sexual intent. *Sex Roles, 15,* 283-298.

Abramson, P. R. (1973). The relationship of the frequency of masturbation to several aspects of personality and behavior. *Journal of Sex Research, 9,* 132-142.

Adams, B. N. (1986). *The family: A sociological interpretation.* Orlando, FL: Harcourt Brace Jovanovich.

Adams, J. S. (1965). Inequity in social exchange. In L. Berkowitz (Ed.), *Advances in experimental social psychology* (Vol. 2, pp. 267-299). New York: Academic Press.

Adelman, M. B. (1991). Play and incongruity: Framing safe-sex talk. *Health Communication, 3,* 139-155.

Adler, N. L., Hendrick, S. S., & Hendrick, C. (1986). Male sexual preference and attitudes toward love and sexuality. *Journal of Sex Education and Therapy, 12,* 27-30.

Allgeier, E. R. (1986, August). *Coercive versus consensual sexual interactions.* Paper presented at the Annual Meetings of the American Psychological Association, Washington, DC.

Allgeier, E. R., & Royster, B. J. T. (1991). New approaches to dating and sexuality. In E. Grauerholz & M. Koralewski (Eds.), *Sexual coercion: Its nature, causes and prevention* (pp. 133-147). Lexington, MA: Lexington.

Altman, I., & Taylor, D. A. (1973). *Social penetration: The development of interpersonal relationships.* New York: Holt, Rinehart & Winston.

Alzate, H. (1984). Sexual behavior of unmarried Colombian university students: A five year follow-up. *Archives of Sexual Behavior, 13,* 121-131.

Angier, N. (1985, January 28). Sexes: Finding trouble in paradise. *Time,* p. 76.

Aron, A., & Aron, E. N. (1991). Love and sexuality. In K. McKinney & S. Sprecher (Eds.), *Sexuality in close relationships* (pp. 25-48). Hillsdale, NJ: Lawrence Erlbaum.

Aron, A., Dutton, D. G., Aron, E. N., & Iverson, A. (1989). Experiences of falling in love. *Journal of Social and Personal Relationships, 6,* 243-257.

Atwater, L. (1982). *The extramarital connection.* New York: Irvington.

Banmen, J., & Vogel, N. A. (1985). The relationship between marital quality and interpersonal sexual communication. *Family Therapy, 12,* 45-58.

Barbach, L., & Geisinger, D. L. (1992). *Going the distance.* New York: Doubleday.

Baron, R. A. (1987). Effects of negative ions on interpersonal attraction: Evidence for intensification. *Journal of Personality and Social Psychology, 52,* 547-553.

Baxter, L. A., & Bullis, C. (1986). Turning points in developing romantic relationships. *Human Communication Research, 12,* 469-493.

Baxter, L. A., & Wilmot, W. W. (1985). Taboo topics in close relationships. *Journal of Social and Personal Relationships, 2,* 253-269.

Bell, A. P., & Weinberg, M. S. (1978). *Homosexualities: A study of diversity among men and women.* New York: Simon & Schuster.

Bell, R. A., Buerkel-Rothfuss, N. L., & Gore, K. E. (1987). "Did you bring the yarmulke for the cabbage patch kid?" The idiomatic communication of young lovers. *Human Communication Research, 14,* 47-67.

Bell, R. A., Daly, J. A., & Gonzalez, C. (1987). Affinity-maintenance in marriage and its relationship to women's marital satisfaction. *Journal of Marriage and the Family, 49,* 445-454.

Bentler, P. M. (1968a). Heterosexual behavior assessment—I, males. *Behavior Research and Therapy, 6,* 21-25.

Bentler, P. M. (1968b). Heterosexual behavior assessment—II, females. *Behavior Research and Therapy, 6,* 27-30.

Berger, C. R. (1987a). Communicating under uncertainty. In M. E. Roloff & G. R. Miller (Eds.), *Interpersonal processes: New directions in communication research* (pp. 39-62). Newbury Park, CA: Sage.

Berger, C. R. (1987b). Planning and scheming: Strategies for initiating relationships. In R. Burnett, P. McChee, & D. Clarke (Eds.), *Accounting for relationships: Explanation, representation and knowledge* (pp. 158-174). New York: Methuen.

Bermant, G. (1976). Sexual behavior: Hard times with the Coolidge effect. In M. H. Siegel & H. P. Zeigler (Eds.), *Psychological research: The inside story.* New York: Harper & Row.

Berscheid, E. (1985). Interpersonal attraction. In G. Lindzey & E. Aronson (Eds.), *Handbook of social psychology* (3rd ed., Vol. 2, pp. 413-484). New York: Random House.

Berscheid, E., Graziano, W., Monson, T., & Dermer, M. (1976). Outcome dependency: Attention, attribution and attraction. *Journal of Personality and Social Psychology, 33,* 709-718.

Berscheid, E., Snyder, M., & Omoto, A. M. (1989). Issues in studying close relationships: Conceptualizing and measuring closeness. In C. Hendrick (Ed.), *Close relationships* (pp. 63-91). Newbury Park, CA: Sage.

Birchler, G. R., & Webb, L. J. (1977). Discriminating interaction behavior in happy and unhappy marriages. *Journal of Consulting and Clinical Psychology, 45,* 494-495.

Bishop, P. D., & Lipsitz, A. (1991). Sexual behavior among college students in the AIDS era: A comparative study. *Journal of Psychology and Human Sexuality, 3,* 35-52.

Blumstein, P., & Schwartz, P. (1983). *American couples.* New York: William Morrow.

Boeringer, S. B., Shehan, C. L., & Akers, R. L. (1991). Social contexts and social learning in sexual coercion and aggression: Assessing the contribution of fraternity membership. *Family Relations, 40,* 58-64.

Bowen, S. P., & Michal-Johnson, P. (1989). The crisis of communicating in relationships: Confronting the threat of AIDS. *AIDS and Public Policy, 4,* 10-19.

Bower, D. W., & Christopher, V. A. (1977). University students' cohabitation: A regional comparison of selected attitudes and behavior. *Journal of Marriage and the Family, 39,* 447-453.

Bowker, L. H. (1983). Marital rape: A distinct syndrome? *Social CaseWork: The Journal of Contemporary Social Work, 64,* 347-352.

Brehm, S. S. (1985). *Intimate relationships.* New York: McGraw-Hill.

Brehm, S. S. (1992). *Intimate relationships* (2nd ed.). New York: McGraw-Hill.

Bressler, L. C., & Lavender, A. D. (1986). Sexual fulfillment of heterosexual, bisexual, and homosexual women. *Journal of Homosexuality, 12,* 109-122.

Bridges, J. S. (1991). Perceptions of date and stranger rape: A difference in sex role expectations and rape supportive beliefs. *Sex Roles, 24,* 291-308.

Bridges, J. S., & McGrail, L. A. (1989). Attributions of responsibility for date and stranger rape. *Sex Roles, 21,* 273-286.

Bringle, R. G., & Buunk, B. P. (1991). Extradyadic relationships and sexual jealousy. In K. McKinney & S. Sprecher (Eds.), *Sexuality in close relationships* (pp. 135-153). Hillsdale, NJ: Lawrence Erlbaum.

Britton, D. M. (1990). Homophobia and homosociality: An analysis of boundary maintenance. *Sociological Quarterly, 3,* 423-439.

Brown, M., & Auerback, A. (1981). Communication patterns in initiation of marital sex. *Medical Aspects of Human Sexuality, 15,* 105-117.

Brown, S. V. (1985). Premarital sexual permissiveness among black adolescent females. *Social Psychology Quarterly, 48,* 381-387.

Burt, M. (1991). Rape myths and acquaintance rape. In A. Parrot & L. Bechhofer (Eds.), *Acquaintance rape: The hidden crime* (pp. 26-40). New York: John Wiley.

Buss, D. M. (1989a). Conflict between the sexes: Strategic interference and the evocation of anger and upset. *Journal of Personality and Social Psychology, 56,* 735-747.

Buss, D. M. (1989b). Love acts: The evolutionary biology of love. In R. J. Sternberg & M. L. Barnes (Eds.), *The psychology of love* (pp. 100-118). New Haven, CT: Yale University Press.

Buss, D. M. (1989c). Sex differences in human mate preferences: Evolutionary hypotheses tested in 37 cultures. *Behavioral and Brain Sciences, 12,* 1-49.

Buss, D. M., & Barnes, M. (1986). Preferences in human mate selection. *Journal of Personality and Social Psychology, 50,* 559-570.

Buunk, B. (1987). Long-term stability and change in sexually open marriages. In L. Shamgar-Handelman & R. Polomba (Eds.), *Alternative patterns of family life in modern societies* (pp. 61-72). Rome, Italy: Istituto di Ricerche sulla Popolazione (Collana Monografie 1).

Byers, E. S., & Heinlein, L. (1989). Predicting initiations and refusals of sexual activities in married and cohabiting heterosexual couples. *Journal of Sex Research, 26,* 210-231.

Byers, E. S., & Lewis, K. (1988). Dating couples' disagreements over the desired level of sexual intimacy. *Journal of Sex Research, 24,* 15-29.

Byrne, D. (1971). *The attraction paradigm.* New York: Academic Press.

Byrne, D. (1977). Sexual changes in society and in science. In D. Byrne & L. A. Byrne (Eds.), *Exploring human sexuality.* New York: Harper & Row.

Byrne, D., & Clore, G. L. (1970). A reinforcement model of evaluative responses. *Personality, 1,* 103-128.

Byrne, D., Ervin, C. E., & Lamberth, J. (1970). Continuity between the experimental study of attraction and real-life computer dating. *Journal of Personality and Social Psychology, 16,* 157-165.

Call, V. R. A., Sprecher, S., & Schwartz, P. (1992, November). *The frequency of sexual intercourse in American couples: A national sample.* Paper presented at the Annual Meeting of the National Council on Family Relations, Orlando, FL.

Carroll, J. L., Volk, K. D., & Hyde, J. S. (1985). Differences between males and females in motives for engaging in sexual intercourse. *Archives of Sexual Behavior, 14,* 131-139.

Carroll, L. (1988). Concern with AIDS and the sexual behavior of college students. *Journal of Marriage and the Family, 50,* 405-411.

Cate, R. M., Lloyd, S. A., Henton, J. M., & Larson, J. H. (1982). Fairness and reward level as predictors of relationship satisfaction. *Social Psychology Quarterly, 45,* 177-181.

Chesney, A. P., Blakeney, P. E., Cole, C., & Chan, F. A. (1981). A comparison of couples who have sought sex therapy with couples who have not. *Journal of Sex and Marital Therapy, 7,* 70-79.

Christopher, F. S. (1988). An initial investigation into a continuum of premarital sexual pressure. *Journal of Sex Research, 25,* 255-266.

Christopher, F. S., & Cate, R. M. (1984). Factors involved in premarital sexual decision-making. *Journal of Sex Research, 20,* 363-376.

Christopher, F. S., & Cate, R. M. (1985a). Anticipated influences on sexual decision-making for first intercourse. *Family Relations, 34,* 265-270.

Christopher, F. S., & Cate, R. M. (1985b). Premarital sexual pathways and relationship development. *Journal of Social and Personal Relationships, 2,* 271-288.

Christopher, F. S., & Cate, R. M. (1988). Premarital sexual involvement: A developmental investigation of relational correlates. *Adolescence, 23,* 793-803.

Christopher, F. S., & Frandsen, M. M. (1990). Strategies of influence in sex and dating. *Journal of Social and Personal Relationships, 7,* 89-105.

Christopher, F. S., London, H. L., & Owens, L. A. (1991, May). *Individual and relational correlates of premarital sexual aggression.* Paper presented at the Third International Network on Personal Relationships Conference, Normal, IL.

Christopher, F. S., Owens, L. A., & Stecker, H. L. (1991, November). *Exploring the darkside of courtship: Male sexual aggression.* Paper presented at the Annual Conference of the National Council on Family Relations, Denver, CO.

Clayton, R. R., & Bokemeier, J. L. (1980). Premarital sex in the seventies. *Journal of Marriage and the Family, 42,* 759-775.

Cleek, M. G., & Pearson, T. A. (1985). Perceived causes of divorce: An analysis of interrelationships. *Journal of Marriage and the Family, 47,* 179-183.

Clement, U. (1990). Surveys of heterosexual behavior. In J. Bancroft, C. M. Davis, & D. Weinstein (Eds.), *Annual review of sex research* (Vol. 1, pp. 45-74). Mt. Vernon, IA: Society for the Scientific Study of Sex.

Cline, R. J., Freeman, K. E., & Johnson, S. J. (1990). Talk among sexual partners about AIDS: Factors differentiating those who talk from those who do not. *Communication Research, 17,* 792-808.

Cline, R. J. W., Johnson, S. J., & Freeman, K. E. (1992). Talk among sexual partners about AIDS: Interpersonal communication for risk reduction or risk enhancement? *Health Communication, 4,* 39-56.

Cochran, S. D., & Mays, V. M. (1990). Sex, lies, and HIV. *New England Journal of Medicine, 322,* 774-775.

Coleman, E. M., Hoon, P. W., & Hoon, E. F. (1983). Arousability and sexual satisfaction in lesbian and heterosexual women. *Journal of Sex Research, 19,* 58-73.

Copenhaver, S., & Grauerholz, E. (1991). Sexual victimization among sorority women: Exploring the link between sexual violence and institutional practices. *Sex Roles, 24,* 31-41.

Cornog, M. (1986). Naming sexual body parts: Preliminary patterns and implications. *Journal of Sex Research, 22,* 393-398.

Craig, M. E., Kalichman, S. C., & Follingstad, D. R. (1989). Verbal coercive sexual behavior among college students. *Archives of Sexual Behavior, 18,* 421-434.

Crooks, R., & Baur, K. (1990). *Our sexuality.* Menlo Park, CA: Benjamin/ Cummings.

Cunningham, M. R. (1989). Reactions to heterosexual opening gambits: Female selectivity and male responsiveness. *Personality and Social Psychology Bulletin, 15,* 27-41.

Cupach, W. R., & Comstock, J. (1990). Satisfaction with sexual communication in marriage: Links to sexual satisfaction and dyadic adjustment. *Journal of Social and Personal Relationships, 7,* 179-186.

Dainton, M. (1991, May). *Relational maintenance revisited: The addition of physical affection measures to a maintenance typology.* Paper presented to the International Communication Association, Chicago, IL.

Darling, C. A., Davidson, J. K., & Cox, R. P. (1991). Female sexual response and the timing of partner orgasm. *Journal of Sex and Marital Therapy, 17,* 3-21.

Darling, C. A., Kallen, D. J., & Van Dusen, J. E. (1984). Sex in transition, 1900-1980. *Journal of Youth and Adolescence, 13,* 385-399.

D'Augelli, J. F., & Cross, H. L. (1975). Relationship of sex guilt and moral reasoning to premarital sex in college women and in couples. *Journal of Consulting and Clinical Psychology, 43,* 40-47.

D'Augelli, J. F., & D'Augelli, A. R. (1977). Moral reasoning and premarital sexual behavior: Toward reasoning about relationships. *Journal of Social Issues, 33,* 44-66.

Davis, C. (1987). *Sexuality related measures: A compendium.* Syracuse, NY: Syracuse University Press.

Davis, J. A. (1980). *General social surveys, 1972-1980: Cumulative data.* Chicago: National Opinion Research Center.

Davis, J. A., & Smith, T. W. (1987). *General social surveys, 1972-1988.* Chicago: National Opinion Research Center.

Degler, C. (1974). What ought to be and what was: Women's sexuality in the nineteenth century. *American Historical Review, 79,* 1467-1490.

Degler, C. (1980). *At odds: Women and the family in America from the Revolution to the present.* New York: Oxford University Press.

DeLamater, J. D. (1989). The social control of human sexuality. In K. McKinney & S. Sprecher (Eds.), *Human sexuality: The societal and interpersonal context* (pp. 30-62). Norwood, NJ: Ablex.

DeLamater, J. D., & MacCorquodale, P. (1979). *Premarital sexuality: Attitudes, relationships, behaviors.* Madison: University of Wisconsin Press.

DeMaris, A., & Rao, K. V. (1990, May). *The frequency of sexual intercourse in intimate relationships.* Paper presented at the Annual Conference of the Population Association of America, Toronto.

Denney, N. W., Field, J. K., & Quadagno, D. (1984). Sex differences in sexual needs and desires. *Archives of Sexual Behavior, 13,* 233-245.

Derlega, V. J., & Berg, J. H. (1987). *Self-disclosure: Theory, research, and therapy.* New York: Plenum.

Derogatis, L. R., & Melisaratos, N. (1979). The DSFI: A multidimensional measure of sexual functioning. *Journal of Sexual and Marital Therapy, 5,* 244-281.

Dignan, M., & Anspaugh, D. (1978). Permissiveness and premarital sexual activity: Behavioral correlates of attitudinal differences. *Adolescence, 13,* 703-711.

Dindia, K. (1988, July). *The marital maintenance survey: Toward the development of a measure of marital maintenance strategies.* Paper presented at the International Conference on Personal Relationships, Vancouver, BC.

Driscoll, R., Davis, K. E., & Lipetz, M. E. (1972). Parental interference and romantic love: The Romeo and Juliet effect. *Journal of Personality and Social Psychology, 24,* 1-10.

Edgar, T., & Fitzpatrick, M. A. (1988). Compliance-gaining in relational interaction: When your life depends on it. *Southern Speech Communication Journal, 53,* 385-405.

Edgar, T., Freimuth, V. S., Hammond, S. L., McDonald, D. A., & Fink, E. L. (1992). Strategic sexual communication: Condom use resistance and response. *Health Communication, 4,* 83-104

Edwards, J. N., & Booth, A. (1976). Sexual behavior in and out of marriage: An assessment of correlates. *Journal of Marriage and the Family, 38,* 73-81.

Eggert, L. L., & Parks, M. R. (1987). Communication network involvement in adolescents' friendship and romantic relationships. In M. L. McLaughlin (Ed.), *Communication yearbook 10* (pp. 283-322). Newbury Park, CA: Sage.

Ehrmann, W. W. (1959). *Premarital dating behavior.* New York: Holt.

Elder, G. H., Jr. (1969). Appearance and education in marriage mobility. *American Sociological Review, 34,* 519-533.

Engel, J. W., & Saracino, M. (1986). Love preferences and ideals: A comparison of homosexual, bisexual, and heterosexual groups. *Contemporary Family Therapy, 8,* 241-250.

Feingold, A. (1990). Gender differences in effects of physical attractiveness on romantic attraction: A comparison across five research paradigms. *Journal of Personality and Social Psychology, 59,* 981-993.

Felmlee, D., Sprecher, S., & Bassin, E. (1990). The dissolution of intimate relationships: A hazard model. *Social Psychology Quarterly, 53,* 13-30.

Fenstermaker, S. (1989). Acquaintance rape on campus: Responsibility and attributions of crime. In M. Pirog-Good & J. Stets (Eds.), *Violence in dating relationships* (pp. 257-281). New York: Praeger.

Ferrell, M. Z., Tolone, W. L., & Walsh, R. H. (1977). Maturational and societal changes in the sexual double-standard: A panel analysis (1967-1971; 1970-1974). *Journal of Marriage and the Family, 39,* 255-271.

Finkelhor, D., & Yllö, K. (1985). *License to rape: Sexual abuse of wives.* New York: Free Press.

Fischer, G. J. (1986). College student attitudes toward forcible date rape: I. Cognitive predictors. *Archives of Sexual Behavior, 15,* 457-466.

Fisher, S. (1973). *The female orgasm.* New York: Basic Books.

Fisher, W. A., White, L. A., Byrne, D., & Kelley, K. (1988). Erotophobia-erotophilia as a dimension of personality. *Journal of Sex Research, 25,* 123-151.

Foa, U. G., & Foa, E. B. (1974). *Societal structures of the mind.* Springfield, IL: Charles C Thomas.

Ford, B. (1980). *Patterns of sex.* New York: St. Martin's.

Frieze, I. (1983). Investigating the causes and consequences of marital rape. *Signs, 8,* 532-553.

Gagnon, J. H. (1975). Sex research and social change. *Archives of Sexual Behavior, 4,* 111-141.

Gagnon, J. H. (1990). The explicit and implicit use of scripting perspective in sex research. In J. Bancroft, C. M. Davis, & D. Weinstein (Eds.), *Annual review of sex research* (Vol. 1, pp. 1-43). Mt. Vernon, IA: Society for the Scientific Study of Sex.

Gagnon, J. H., & Simon, W. (1973). *Sexual conduct: The social sources of human sexuality.* Hawthorne, NY: Aldine.

Gagnon, J. H., & Simon, W. (1987). The sexual scripting of oral-genital contacts. *Archives of Sexual Behavior, 16,* 1-25.

Gangestad, S. W., & Simpson, J. A. (1990). Toward an evolutionary history of female sociosexual variation. *Journal of Personality, 58,* 69-96.

Garcia, L. (1983). Sexual stereotypes and attributions about sexual arousal. *Journal of Sex Research, 19,* 366-375.

Garcia, L., Milano, L., & Quijano, A. (1989). Perceptions of coercive sexual behavior by males and females. *Sex Roles, 21,* 569-577.

Gaulier, B., Travis, S. K., & Allgeier, E. R. (1986). *Proceptive behavior and the use of behavioral cues in heterosexual courtship.* Paper presented at the Annual Meeting of the Midcontinent Region of the Society for the Scientific Study of Sex, Madison, WI.

Geer, J. H., & Broussard, D. B. (1990). Scaling heterosexual behavior and arousal: Consistency and sex differences. *Journal of Personality and Social Psychology, 58,* 664-671.

Gerdes, E. P., Dammann, E. J., & Heilig, K. E. (1988). Perceptions of rape victims and assailants: Effects of physical attractiveness, acquaintance, and subject gender. *Sex Roles, 19,* 141-153.

Gergen, K. J. (1973). Social psychology as history. *Journal of Personality and Social Psychology, 26,* 309-320.

Giarrusso, R., Johnson, P. B., Goodchilds, J., & Zellman, G. (1979, April). *Adolescents' cues and signals: Sex and assault.* Paper presented at the Western Psychological Association Meetings, San Diego, CA.

Gidycz, C. A., & Koss, M. P. (1991). The effects of acquaintance rape on the female victim. In A. Parrot & L. Bechhofer (Eds.), *Acquaintance rape: The hidden crime* (pp. 270-284). New York: John Wiley.

Glenn, N. D., & Weaver, C. N. (1979). Attitudes toward premarital, extramarital and homosexual relations in the U.S. in the 70's. *Journal of Sex Research, 15,* 108-118.

Grauerholz, E., & Serpe, R. T. (1985). Initiation and response: The dynamics of sexual interaction. *Sex Roles, 12,* 1041-1059.

Grauerholz, E., & Solomon, J. C. (1989). Sexual coercion: Power and violence. In K. McKinney & S. Sprecher (Eds.), *Human sexuality: The societal and interpersonal context* (pp. 350-369). Norwood, NJ: Ablex.

Gray, L. A., & Saracino, M. (1991). College students' attitudes, beliefs, and behaviors about AIDS: Implications for family life educators. *Family Relations, 40,* 258-263.

Greeley, A. M. (1991). *Faithful attraction: Discovering intimacy, love, and fidelity in American marriage.* New York: Doherty.

Green, S. K., & Sandos, P. (1983). Perceptions of male and female initiators of relationships. *Sex Roles, 9,* 849-852.

Greenblat, C. S. (1983). The salience of sexuality in the early years of marriage. *Journal of Marriage and the Family, 45,* 289-299.

Gregersen, E. (1983). *Sexual practices: The story of human sexuality.* New York: Franklin Watts.

Griffiths, S. (1971). Rape: The all-American crime. *Ramparts, 10,* 335-381.

Griffitt, W. (1970). Environmental effects on interpersonal affective behavior: Ambient effective temperature and attraction. *Journal of Personality and Social Psychology, 15,* 240-244.

Griffitt, W., & Veitch, R. (1971). Hot and crowded: Influence of population density and temperature on interpersonal affective behavior. *Journal of Personality and Social Psychology, 17,* 92-98.

Grosskopf, D. (1983). *Sex and the married woman.* New York: Simon & Schuster.

Halpern, J., & Sherman, M. A. (1979). *Afterplay: A key to intimacy.* New York: Pocket Books.

Hampe, G. D., & Ruppel, H. J. (1974). The measurement of premarital sexual permissiveness: A comparison of two Guttman scales. *Journal of Marriage and the Family, 36,* 451-463.

Harney, P. A., & Muehlenhard, C. L. (1991). Rape. In E. Grauerholz & M. A. Koralewski (Eds.), *Sexual coercion: A source book on its nature, causes, and prevention* (pp. 3-15). Lexington, MA: Lexington.

Harrison, A., & Saeed, L. (1977). Let's make a deal: An analysis of revelations and stipulations in lonely hearts advertisements. *Journal of Personality and Social Psychology, 35,* 257-264.

Harrison, D. E., Bennett, W. H., Globetti, G., & Alsikafi, M. (1974). Premarital sexual standards of rural youth. *Journal of Sex Research, 10,* 266-277.

Hart, B. (1986). Lesbian battering: An examination. In K. Lobel (Ed.), *Naming the violence: Speaking out about lesbian battering* (pp. 173-189). Seattle: Seal.

Harvey, J. H., Flanary, R., & Morgan, M. (1986). Vivid memories of vivid loves gone by. *Journal of Social and Personal Relationships, 3,* 359-373.

Hatfield, E., Greenberger, D., Traupmann, J., & Lambert, P. (1982). Equity and sexual satisfaction in recently married couples. *Journal of Sex Research, 18,* 18-32.

Hatfield, E., & Rapson, R. (1993). *Love, sex, and intimacy: Their psychology, biology, and history.* New York: Harper Collins.

Hatfield, E., & Sprecher, S. (1986a). Measuring passionate love in intimate relationships. *Journal of Adolescence, 9,* 383-410.

Hatfield, E., & Sprecher, S. (1986b). *Mirror, mirror . . . The importance of looks in everyday life.* Albany: State University of New York Press.

Hatfield, E., Sprecher, S., Pillemer, J. T., Greenberger, D., & Wexler, P. (1988). Gender differences in what is desired in the sexual relationship. *Journal of Psychology and Human Sexuality, 1,* 39-52.

Hatfield, E., & Walster, G. W. (1978). *A new look at love.* Lantham, MA: University Press of America.

Hendrick, C., & Hendrick, S. S. (1988). Lovers wear rose colored glasses. *Journal of Social and Personal Relationships, 5,* 161-183.

Hendrick, S. S., & Hendrick, C. (1987a). Love and sex attitudes: A close relationship. In W. H. Jones & D. Perlman (Eds.), *Advances in personal relationships* (pp. 141-169). Greenwich, CT: JAI.

Hendrick, S. S., & Hendrick, C. (1987b). Love and sexual attitudes, self-disclosure, and sensation-seeking. *Journal of Social and Personal Relationships, 4,* 281-297.

Hendrick, S. S., & Hendrick, C. (1987c). Multidimensionality of sexual attitudes. *Journal of Sex Research, 23,* 502-526.

Hendrick, S. S., & Hendrick, C. (1992). *Liking, loving, and relating* (2nd ed.). Belmont, CA: Brooks/Cole.

Hendrick, S. S., Hendrick, C., Slapion-Foote, M. J., & Foote, F. H. (1985). Gender differences in sexual attitudes. *Journal of Personality and Social Psychology, 48,* 1630-1642.

Henze, L. F., & Hudson, J. W. (1969). Campus values in mate selection: A replication. *Journal of Marriage and the Family, 31,* 772-775.

Herek, G. M. (1984). Attitudes toward lesbians and gay men: A factor-analytic study. *Journal of Homosexuality, 10,* 39-52.

Herold, E. S., & Goodwin, M. S. (1981). Adamant virgins, potential nonvirgins and nonvirgins. *Journal of Sex Research, 17,* 97-113.

Hessellund, H. (1976). Masturbation and sexual fantasies in married couples. *Archives of Sexual Behavior, 5,* 133-147.

Hill, C. T., Rubin, Z., & Peplau, L. A. (1976). Breakups before marriage: The end of 103 affairs. *Journal of Social Issues, 32,* 147-168.

Hill, R. (1945). Campus values in mate selection. *Journal of Home Economics, 37,* 554-558.

Hite, S. (1976). *The Hite report.* New York: Dell.

Hite, S. (1981). *The Hite report on male sexuality.* New York: Knopf.

Homans, G. C. (1961). *Social behavior.* New York: Harcourt, Brace & World.

Hoon, E. F., Hoon, P. W., & Wincze, J. P. (1976). An inventory for the measurement of female sexual arousability: The SAI. *Archives of Sexual Behavior, 5,* 291-300.

Howard, J. A., Blumstein, P., & Schwartz, P. (1987). Social or evolutionary theories? Some observations on preferences in human mate selection. *Journal of Personality and Social Psychology, 53,* 194-200.

Hoyt, L. L., & Hudson, J. W. (1981). Personal characteristics important in mate preference among college students. *Social Behavior and Personality, 9,* 93-96.

Hudson, W. W., Harrison, D. F., & Crosscup, P. C. (1981). A short-form scale to measure sexual discord in dyadic relationships. *Journal of Sex Research, 17,* 157-174.

Hudson, W. W., & Ricketts, W. A. (1980). A strategy for the measurement of homophobia. *Journal of Homosexuality, 5,* 357-372.

Hunt, M. (1974). *Sexual behavior in the 1970's.* Chicago: Playboy Press.

Hurlbert, D. F. (1991). The role of assertiveness in female sexuality: A comparative study between sexually assertive and sexually nonassertive women. *Journal of Sex and Marital Therapy, 17,* 183-190.

Hurlbert, D. F., & Whittaker, K. E. (1991). The role of masturbation in marital and sexual satisfaction: A comparative study of female masturbators and nonmasturbators. *Journal of Sex Education and Therapy, 17,* 272-282.

Huston, T. L., Surra, C., Fitzgerald, N. M., & Cate, R. (1981). From courtship to marriage: Mate selection as an interpersonal process. In S. Duck & R. Gilmour (Eds.), *Personal relationships 2: Developing personal relationships* (pp. 53-88). New York: Academic Press.

Huston, T. L., & Vangelisti, A. L. (1991). Socioemotional behavior and satisfaction in marital relationships: A longitudinal study. *Journal of Personality and Social Psychology, 61,* 721-733.

Hyde, J. S. (1990). *Understanding human sexuality.* New York: McGraw-Hill.

Istvan, J., & Griffitt, W. (1980). Effects of sexual experience on dating desirability and marriage desirability: An experimental study. *Journal of Marriage and the Family, 42,* 377-385.

Iwawaki, S., & Eysenck, H. J. (1978). Sexual attitudes among British and Japanese students. *Journal of Psychology, 98,* 289-298.

Jacoby, A. P., & Williams, J. D. (1985). Effects of premarital sexual standards and behavior on dating and marriage desirability. *Journal of Marriage and the Family, 47,* 1059-1065.

James, W. H. (1974). Marital coital rates, spouses' ages, family size, and social class. *Journal of Sex Research, 10,* 205-218.

James, W. H. (1981). The honeymoon effect on marital coitus. *Journal of Sex Research, 17,* 114-123.

James, W. H. (1983). Decline in coital rates with spouses' ages and duration of marriage. *Journal of Biosocial Science, 15,* 83-87.

Jemail, J. A., & Geer, J. H. (1977). Sexual scripts. In R. Gemme & C. Wheeler (Eds.), *Progress in sexology* (pp. 513-522). New York: Plenum.

Jensen, G. D. (1978). Masturbation by married men. *Archives of Sexual Behavior, 12,* 37.

Jesser, C. J. (1978). Male responses to direct verbal sexual initiatives of females. *Journal of Sex Research, 14,* 118-128.

Johnson, D. J., & Rusbult, C. E. (1989). Resisting temptation: Devaluation of alternative partners as a means of maintaining commitment in close relationships. *Journal of Personality and Social Psychology, 57,* 967-980.

Johnson, J. D., & Jackson, L. A. (1988). Assessing the effects of factors that might underlie the differential perception of acquaintance and stranger rape. *Sex Roles, 19,* 37-45.

Johnson, R. E. (1970). Extramarital sexual intercourse: A methodological note. *Journal of Marriage and the Family, 32,* 279-283.

Kaats, G. R., & Davis, K. E. (1970). The dynamics of sexual behavior of college students. *Journal of Marriage and the Family, 32,* 390-399.

Kanin, E. J. (1957). Male aggression in dating-courtship relations. *American Journal of Sociology, 63,* 197-204.

Kanin, E. J. (1969). Selected dyadic aspects of male sexual aggression. *Journal of Sex Research, 5,* 12-28.

Kanin, E. J. (1984). Date rape: Unofficial criminals and victims. *Victimology: An International Journal, 9,* 95-108.

Kanin, E. J., & Parcell, S. R. (1977). Sexual aggression: A second look at the offended female. *Archives of Sexual Behavior, 6,* 67-76.

Kantner, J., & Zelnick, M. (1972). Sexual experience of young unmarried women in the United States. *Family Planning Perspectives, 4,* 9-18.

Kelley, H., Berscheid, E., Christensen, A., Harvey, J., Huston, T., Levinger, G., McClintock, E., Peplau, L., & Peterson, D. (1983). Analyzing close relationships. In H. Kelley, E. Berscheid, A. Christensen, J. Harvey, T. Huston, G. Levinger, E. McClintock, L. Peplau, & D. Peterson (Eds.), *Close relationships* (pp. 20-67). San Francisco: Freeman.

Kelley, K., Pilchowicz, E., & Byrne, D. (1981). Responses of males to female-initiated dates. *Bulletin of the Psychonomic Society, 17,* 195-196.

Kenrick, D. T., Sadalla, E. K., Groth, G., & Trost, M. R. (1990). Evolution, traits, and the stages of human courtship: Qualifying the parental investment model. *Journal of Personality, 58,* 97-116.

Kenrick, D. T., & Trost, M. R. (1989). A reproductive exchange model of heterosexual relationships. In C. Hendrick (Ed.), *Close relationships* (pp. 92-118). Newbury Park, CA: Sage.

Kenrick, D. T., Trost, M. R., Groth, G., & Sadalla, E. K. (1988). *Gender differences in mate selection criteria vary with different phases of courtship.* Unpublished manuscript.

Kerckhoff, A. C. (1974). The social context of interpersonal attraction. In T. L. Huston (Ed.), *Foundations of interpersonal attraction* (pp. 61-78). New York: Academic Press.

Kilpatrick, D. G., Best, C. L., Veronen, L. J., Amick, A. E., Villeponteaus, L. A., & Ruff, G. A. (1985). Mental health correlates of criminal victimization: A random community survey. *Journal of Consulting and Clinical Psychology, 53,* 866-873.

King, H. E., & Webb, C. (1981). Rape crisis centers: Progress and problems. *Journal of Social Issues, 37,* 93-104.

King, K., Balswick, J. O., & Robinson, I. E. (1977). The continuing premarital sexual revolution among college females. *Journal of Marriage and the Family, 39,* 455-459.

Kinsey, A. C., Pomeroy, W. B., & Martin, C. E. (1948). *Sexual behavior in the human male.* Philadelphia: W. B. Saunders.

Kinsey, A. C., Pomeroy, W. B., Martin, C. E., & Gephard, P. H. (1953). *Sexual behavior in the human female.* Philadelphia: W. B. Saunders.

Kirkpatrick, C. (1980). Sex roles and sexual satisfaction in women. *Psychology of Women Quarterly, 4,* 444-459.

Kirkpatrick, C., & Kanin, E. (1957). Male sex aggression on a university campus. *American Sociological Review, 22,* 52-58.

Kite, M. E., & Deaux, K. (1986). Attitudes toward homosexuality: Assessment and behavioral consequences. *Basic and Applied Social Psychology, 7,* 137-162.

Kleinke, C. L., Meeker, F. B., & Staneski, R. A. (1986). Preference for opening lines: Comparing ratings by men and women. *Sex Roles, 15,* 585-600.

Klemmack, D. L., & Roff, L. L. (1980). Heterosexual alternatives to marriage: Appropriateness for older persons. *Alternative Lifestyles, 3,* 137-148.

Knox, D., & Wilson, K. (1981). Dating behaviors of university students. *Family Relations, 30,* 255-258.

Koestner, R., & Wheeler, L. (1988). Self-presentation in personal advertisements: The influence of implicit notions of attraction and role expectations. *Journal of Social and Personal Relationships, 5,* 149-160.

Korman, S. K., & Leslie, G. R. (1982). The relationship of feminist ideology and date expense sharing to perceptions of sexual aggression in dating. *Journal of Sex Research, 18,* 114-129.

Koss, M. P. (1988). Hidden rape: Incidence, prevalence, and descriptive characteristics of sexual aggression and victimization in a national sample of college students. In W. A. Burgess (Ed.), *Sexual assault* (Vol. 2, pp. 1-25). New York: Garland.

Koss, M. P., Dinero, T. E., Seibel, C. A., & Cox, S. (1988). Stranger and acquaintance rape: Are there differences in the victim's experience? *Psychology of Women Quarterly, 12,* 1-24.

Koss, M. P., Gidycz, C. A., & Wisniewski, N. (1987). The scope of rape: Incidence and prevalence of sexual aggression and victimization in a national sample of higher education students. *Journal of Consulting and Clinical Psychology, 55,* 162-170.

Koss, M. P., & Oros, C. J. (1982). Sexual experiences survey: A research instrument investigating sexual aggression and victimization. *Journal of Consulting and Clinical Psychology, 50,* 455-457.

Kurdek, L. A. (1988). Relationship quality of gay and lesbian cohabitating couples. *Journal of Homosexuality, 15,* 93-118.

Kurdek, L. A. (1991a). The dissolution of gay and lesbian couples. *Journal of Social and Personal Relationships, 8,* 265-278.

Kurdek, L. A. (1991b). Sexuality in homosexual and heterosexual couples. In K. McKinney & S. Sprecher (Eds.), *Sexuality in close relationships* (pp. 177-191). Hillsdale, NJ: Lawrence Erlbaum.

LaBeff, E. E., & Dodder, R. A. (1982). Attitudes toward sexual permissiveness in Mexico and the United States. *Journal of Social Psychology, 116,* 285-286.

Laner, M. R. (1977). Permanent partner priorities: Gay and straight. *Journal of Homosexuality, 3,* 21-39.

Laner, M. R., Laner, R. H., & Palmer, C. E. (1978). Permissiveness attitudes toward sexual behaviors: A clarification of theoretical explanations. *Journal of Sex Research, 14,* 137-144.

Lawrance, L., Rubinson, L., & O'Rourke, T. (1984). Sexual attitudes and behaviors: Trends for a ten-year period 1972-1982. *Journal of Sex Education and Therapy, 10,* 22-29.

Lawson, A., & Samson, L. (1988). Age, gender and adultery. *British Journal of Sociology, 39,* 409-440.

Lee, J. A. (1973). *The colors of love: An exploration of the ways of loving.* Don Mills, Ontario: New Press.

Leigh, B. C. (1989). Reasons for having and avoiding sex: Gender, sexual orientation, and relationship to sexual behavior. *Journal of Sex Research, 26,* 199-209.

Levin, R., & Levin, A. (1975, October). Sexual pleasure: The surprising preferences of 100,000 women. *Redbook,* pp. 38, 40, 42, 44, 190, 192.

Levine, E. M., & Kanin, E. J. (1987). Sexual violence among dates and acquaintances: Trends and their implications for marriage and family. *Journal of Family Violence, 2,* 55-65.

Levinger, G. (1970). Husbands' and wives' estimates of coital frequency. *Medical Aspects of Human Sexuality, 4,* 42.

Levinger, G., & Snoek, J. D. (1972). *Attraction in relationship: A new look at interpersonal attraction.* Morristown, NJ: General Learning.

Lewis, C. (1988, May). Date rape is O.K., grade schoolers say. *Philadelphia Inquirer,* p. A-3.

Lewis, R. (1973). Social reactions and the formation of dyads: An interactionist approach to mate selection. *Sociometry, 36,* 409-418.

Libby, R. W., Gray, L., & White, M. (1978). A test and reformulation of reference group and role correlates of premarital sexual permissiveness theory. *Journal of Marriage and the Family, 40,* 79-92.

Lloyd, S. (1991). The darkside of courtship: Violence and sexual exploitation. *Family Relations, 40,* 14-20.

LoPiccolo, J., & Steger, J. C. (1974). The sexual interaction inventory: A new instrument for assessment of sexual dysfunction. *Archives of Sexual Behavior, 3,* 585.

Lundberg-Love, P., & Geffner, R. (1989). Date rape: Prevalence, risk factors, and a proposed model. In M. A. Pirog-Good & J. E. Stets (Eds.), *Violence in dating relationships* (pp. 169-182). New York: Praeger.

Mahoney, E. R. (1978). Gender and social class differences in changes in attitudes toward premarital coitus. *Sociology and Social Research, 62,* 279-288.

Mahoney, E. R. (1980). Religiosity and sexual behavior among heterosexual college students. *Journal of Sex Research, 16,* 97-113.

Malamuth, N., Sockloskie, R., Koss, M., & Tanaka, K. (1991). Characteristics of aggressors against women: Testing a model using a national sample of college students. *Journal of Consulting and Clinical Psychology, 59,* 670-681.

Margolin, L. (1989). Gender and the prerogatives of dating and marriage: An experimental assessment of a sample of college students. *Sex Roles, 20,* 91-102.

Margolin, L., & White, L. (1987). The continuing role of physical attractiveness in marriage. *Journal of Marriage and the Family, 49,* 21-27.

Mark, M., & Miller, M. L. (1986). The effects of sexual permissiveness, target gender, subject gender, and attitude toward women on social perception: In search of the double standard. *Sex Roles, 15,* 311-322.

Martin, P., & Hummer, R. (1989). Fraternities and rape on campus. *Gender and Society, 3,* 457-473.

Marwell, G., McKinney, K., Sprecher, S., DeLamater, J., & Smith, S. (1982, July). *Legitimizing factors in the initiation of heterosexual relationships.* Paper presented at the First International Conference on Personal Relationships, Madison, WI.

Masters, W. H., & Johnson, V. E. (1966). *Human sexual response.* Boston: Little, Brown.

Masters, W. H., & Johnson, V. E. (1970). *Human sexual inadequacy.* Boston: Little, Brown.

Masters, W. H., & Johnson, V. E. (1979). *Homosexuality in perspective.* Boston: Little, Brown.

Masters, W. H., Johnson, V. E., & Kolodny, R. (1986). *Sex and human loving.* Boston: Little, Brown.

May, J. L., & Hamilton, P. A. (1980). Effects of musically evoked affect on women's interpersonal attraction toward and perceptual judgments of physical attractiveness for men. *Motivation and Emotion, 4,* 217-228.

McCabe, M. P. (1987). Desired and experienced levels of premarital affection and sexual intercourse during dating. *Journal of Sex Research, 23,* 23-33.

McCabe, M. P., & Collins, J. K. (1983). The sexual and affectual attitudes and experiences of Australian adolescents during dating: The effects of age, church attendance, type of school, and socioeconomic class. *Archives of Sexual Behavior, 12,* 525-539.

McClosky, H. B., & Brill, A. (1983). *Dimensions of tolerance: What Americans believe about civil liberties.* New York: Russell Sage.

McCormick, N. B. (1979). Come-ons and put-offs: Unmarried students' strategies for having and avoiding sexual intercourse. *Psychology of Women Quarterly, 4,* 194-211.

McGinnis, R. (1959). Campus values in mate selection: A repeat study. *Social Forces, 36,* 368-373.

Mercer, G. W., & Kohn, P. M. (1979). Gender differences in the integration of conservatism, sex urge, and sexual behaviors among college students. *Journal of Sex Research, 15,* 129-142.

Metts, S., & Cupach, W. R. (1991, May). *Plans for seeking and resisting the use of condoms.* Paper presented at the International Communication Association Convention, Chicago, IL.

Metts, S., Cupach, W. R., & Imahori, T. T. (1992). Perceptions of sexual compliance-resisting messages in three types of cross-sex relationships. *Western Journal of Speech Communication, 56,* 1-17.

Metts, S., & Fitzpatrick, M. A. (1992). Thinking about safer sex: The risky business of "know your partner" advice. In T. Edgar, M. A. Fitzpatrick, & V. S. Friemuth (Eds.), *AIDS: A communication perspective* (pp. 1-19). Hillsdale, NJ: Lawrence Erlbaum.

Michaels, J. W., Acock, A. C., & Edwards, J. N. (1986). Social exchange and equity determinants of relationship commitment. *Journal of Social and Personal Relationships, 3,* 161-175.

Miller, B., & Marshall, J. C. (1987, January). Coercive sex on the university campus. *Journal of College Student Personnel,* pp. 38-47.

Millham, J., San Miguel, C. L., & Kellog, R. (1976). A factor-analytic conceptualization of attitudes toward male and female homosexuals. *Journal of Homosexuality, 2,* 3-10.

Moore, M. M. (1985). Nonverbal courtship patterns in women: Context and consequences. *Ethology and Sociobiology, 6,* 237-247.

Morokoff, P. J. (1986). Volunteer bias in the psycho-physiological study of female sexuality. *Journal of Sex Research, 22,* 35-51.

Muehlenhard, C. L. (1988). "Nice women" don't say yes and "real men" don't say no: How miscommunication and the double standard can cause sexual problems. *Women and Therapy, 7,* 95-108.

Muehlenhard, C. L., & Cook, S. W. (1988). Men's reports of unwanted sexual activity. *Journal of Sex Research, 24,* 58-72.

Muehlenhard, C. L., & Dorsey, M. T. (1987, November). *Sex differences in signaling interest: Women's and men's cues that signal interest in dating and friendship.* Paper presented at the Annual Meeting of the Association for Advancement of Behavior Therapy, Boston, MA.

Muehlenhard, C. L., & Falcon, P. L. (1990). Men's heterosexual skill and attitudes toward women as predictors of verbal sexual coercion and forceful rape. *Sex Roles, 23,* 241-259.

Muehlenhard, C. L., Friedman, D. E., & Thomas, C. M. (1985). Is date rape justifiable? *Psychology of Women Quarterly, 9,* 297-310.

Muehlenhard, C. L., Goggins, M. F., Jones, J. M., & Satterfield, A. T. (1991). Sexual violence and coercion in close relationships. In K. McKinney & S. Sprecher (Eds.), *Sexuality in close relationships* (pp. 155-175). Hillsdale, NJ: Lawrence Erlbaum.

Muehlenhard, C. L., & Hollabaugh, L. C. (1988). Do women sometimes say no when they mean yes? The prevalence and correlates of women's token resistance to sex. *Journal of Personality and Social Psychology, 54,* 872-879.

Muehlenhard, C. L., & Linton, M. A. (1987). Date rape and sexual aggression in dating situations: Incidence and risk factors. *Journal of Consulting Psychology, 34,* 186-196.

Muehlenhard, C. L., Linton, M. A., Felts, A. S., & Andrews, S. L. (1985, June). Men's attitudes toward the justifiability of date rape: Intervening variables and possible solutions. In E. Allgeier (Chair), *Sexual coercion: Political issues and empirical findings.* Symposium conducted at the Annual Mid-continent Meeting of the Society for the Scientific Study of Sex, Chicago, IL.

Muehlenhard, C. L., & MacNaughton, J. S. (1988). Women's beliefs about women who "lead men on." *Journal of Social and Clinical Psychology, 7,* 65-79.

Muehlenhard, C. L., & McCoy, M. L. (1991). Double standard/double bind: The sexual double standard and women's communication about sex. *Psychology of Women Quarterly, 15,* 447-461.

Muehlenhard, C. L., & Quackenbush, D. M. (1988, November). *Can the sexual double standard put women at risk for sexually transmitted diseases? The role of the double standard in condom use among women.* Paper presented at the Annual Meeting of the Society for the Scientific Study of Sex, San Francisco, CA.

Murnen, S. K., Perot, A., & Byrne, D. (1989). Coping with unwanted sexual activity: Normative responses, situational components, and individual differences. *Journal of Sex Research, 26,* 85-106.

Murstein, B. I. (1970). Stimulus-value-role: A theory of marital choice. *Journal of Marriage and the Family, 32,* 465-481.

Murstein, B. I. (1986). *Paths to marriage.* Beverly Hills, CA: Sage.

Nevid, J. S. (1984). Sex differences in factors of romantic attraction. *Sex Roles, 11,* 401-411.

Newcomb, M. D. (1983). Relationship qualities of those who live together. *Alternative Lifestyles, 6,* 78-102.

Newcomb, T. M. (1961). *The acquaintance process.* New York: Holt, Rinehart & Winston.

Newcomer, S. F., & Udry, J. R. (1985). Oral sex in an adolescent population. *Archives of Sexual Behavior, 14,* 41-46.

Oliver, M. B., & Sedikides, C. (1992). Effects of sexual permissiveness on desirability of partner as a function of low and high commitment to relationship. *Social Psychology Quarterly, 55,* 321-333.

Omoto, A. M., Berscheid, E., & Snyder, M. (1987, August). *Behavioral and psychological correlates of sexual intercourse in romantic relationships.* Paper presented at the Annual Meeting of the American Psychological Association, New York, NY.

Orbuch, T. L., & Harvey, J. H. (1991). Methodological and conceptual issues in the study of sexuality in close relationships. In K. McKinney & S. Sprecher (Eds.), *Sexuality in close relationships* (pp. 9-24). Hillsdale, NJ: Lawrence Erlbaum.

Padilla, E. R., & O'Grady, K. E. (1987). Sexuality among Mexican Americans: A case of sexual stereotyping. *Journal of Personality and Social Psychology, 52*, 5-10.

Pagelow, M. D. (1988). Marital rape. In V. van Hasselt (Ed.), *Handbook of family violence* (pp. 207-232). New York: Plenum.

Parks, M. R., & Adelman, M. B. (1983). Communication networks and the development of romantic relationships: An expansion of uncertainty reduction theory. *Human Communication Research, 10*, 55-79.

Parks, M. R., & Eggert, L. L. (1991). The role of social context in the dynamics of personal relationships. In W. Jones & D. Perlman (Eds.), *Advances in personal relationships* (Vol. 2, pp. 1-34). London: Jessica Kingsley.

Parven, T. (1883). Hygiene of the sexual functions. *New Orleans Medical and Surgical Journal, 11*, 92-95.

Paxton, A. L., & Turner, E. J. (1978). Self-actualization and sexual permissiveness, satisfaction, prudishness, and drive among female undergraduates. *Journal of Sex Research, 14*, 65-80.

People. (1992, January 13). p. 36.

Peplau, L. A., & Cochran, S. (1981). Value orientations in the intimate relationships of gay men. *Journal of Homosexuality, 6*, 1-9.

Peplau, L. A., Cochran, S., Rook, K., & Padesky, C. (1978). Loving women: Attachment and autonomy in lesbian relationships. *Journal of Social Issues, 34*, 7-27.

Peplau, L. A., & Gordon, S. L. (1983). The intimate relationships of lesbians and gay men. In E. R. Allgeier & N. B. McCormick (Eds.), *Changing boundaries: Gender roles and sexual behavior* (pp. 226-244). Palo Alto, CA: Mayfield.

Peplau, L. A., Padesky, C., & Hamilton, M. (1982). Satisfaction in lesbian relationships. *Journal of Homosexuality, 8*, 23-35.

Peplau, L. A., Rubin, Z., & Hill, C. T. (1977). Sexual intimacy in dating relationships. *Journal of Social Issues, 33*, 86-109.

Perlman, S. D., & Abramson, P. R. (1982). Sexual satisfaction among married and cohabiting individuals. *Journal of Consulting and Clinical Psychology, 50*, 458-460.

Perper, T., & Fox, V. S. (1980, April). *Flirtation behavior in public settings.* Paper presented at the meeting of the Eastern Region of the Society for the Scientific Study of Sex, Philadelphia, PA.

Perper, T., & Weis, D. L. (1987). Proceptive and rejective strategies of U.S. and Canadian college women. *Journal of Sex Research, 23*, 455-480.

Pinney, E. M., Gerrard, M., & Denney, N. W. (1987). The Pinney Sexual Satisfaction Inventory. *Journal of Sex Research, 23*, 233-251.

Poppen, P. J., & Segal, N. J. (1988). The influence of sex and sex role orientation on sexual coercion. *Sex Roles, 19*, 689-702.

Prather, J. E. (1990). "It's just as easy to marry a rich man as a poor one!": Students' accounts of parental messages about marital partners. *Mid-American Review of Sociology, 14,* 151-162.

Prins, K. S., Buunk, B. P., & VanYperen, N. W. (1991, May). *Equity, normative disapproval and extramarital relationships.* Paper presented at the Third International Network Conference on Personal Relationships, Normal/Bloomington, IL.

Rabehl, S. M., Ridge, R. D., & Berscheid, E. (1992). *"Love"* vs. *"In love."* Manuscript submitted for publication.

Rainwater, L. (1966). Some aspects of lower-class sexual behavior. *Journal of Social Issues, 22,* 96-108.

Randolph, B. J., & Winstead, B. (1988). Sexual decision making and object relations theory. *Archives of Sexual Behavior, 17,* 389-409.

Reddon, J. R., Patton, D., & Waring, E. M. (1985). The item-factor structure of the Waring Intimacy Questionnaire. *Educational and Psychological Measurement, 45,* 233-244.

Reiss, I. L. (1960). *Premarital sexual standards in America.* New York: Free Press.

Reiss, I. L. (1964). The scaling of premarital sexual permissiveness. *Journal of Marriage and the Family, 26,* 188-198.

Reiss, I. L. (1967). *The social context of premarital sexual permissiveness.* New York: Holt, Rinehart & Winston.

Reiss, I. L. (1989). Society and sexuality: A sociological explanation. In K. McKinney & S. Sprecher (Eds.), *Human sexuality: The societal and interpersonal context* (pp. 3-29). Norwood, NJ: Ablex.

Reiss, I. L., Anderson, R. E., & Sponaugle, G. C. (1980). A multivariate model of determinants of extramarital permissiveness. *Journal of Marriage and the Family, 42,* 395-411.

Reiss, I. L., & Lee, G. R. (1988). *Family systems in America* (4th ed.). New York: Holt, Rinehart & Winston.

Rhyne, D. (1981). Bases of marital satisfaction among men and women. *Journal of Marriage and the Family, 43,* 941-955.

Riggio, R. E. (1986). Assessment of basic social skills. *Journal of Personality and Social Psychology, 51,* 649-660.

Riggio, R. E., & Zimmerman, J. (1991). Social skills and interpersonal relationships: Influences on social support and support seeking. In W. H. Jones & D. L. Perlman (Eds.), *Advances in personal relationships* (Vol. 2, pp. 133-155). London: Jessica Kingsley.

Riportella-Muller, R. (1989). Sexuality in the elderly: A review. In K. McKinney & S. Sprecher (Eds.), *Human sexuality: The societal and interpersonal context* (pp. 210-236). Norwood, NJ: Ablex.

Risman, B. J., Hill, C., Rubin, Z., & Peplau, L. A. (1981). Living together in college: Implications for courtship. *Journal of Marriage and the Family, 43,* 77-83.

Robinson, I., & Jedlicka, D. (1982). Change in sexual attitudes and behavior of college students from 1965-1980: A research note. *Journal of Marriage and the Family, 44,* 237-240.

Robinson, I., Ziss, K., Ganza, B., & Katz, S. (1991). Twenty years of the sexual revolution, 1965-1985: An update. *Journal of Marriage and the Family, 53,* 216-220.

Robinson, P. A. (1976). *The modernization of sex.* New York: Harper & Row.

Roche, J. P. (1986). Premarital sex: Attitudes and behavior by dating state. *Adolescence, 21,* 107-121.

Rose, S., & Frieze, I. H. (1989). Young singles' scripts for a first date. *Gender & Society, 3,* 258-268.

Rosenbaum, M. E. (1986). The repulsion hypothesis: On the nondevelopment of relationships. *Journal of Personality and Social Psychology, 51,* 1156-1166.

Rubin, L. B. (1976). *Worlds of pain: Life in the working-class family.* New York: Basic Books. Reprinted in Rubin, L. B. (1989). Blue-collar marriage and the sexual revolution. In A. S. Skolnick & J. H. Solnick (Eds.), *Family in transition* (6th ed.), Glenview, IL: Scott Foresman.

Rubin, L. B. (1990). *Erotic wars: What happened to the sexual revolution?* New York: Harper Collins.

Rubin, Z. (1970). Measurement of romantic love. *Journal of Personality and Social Psychology, 16,* 265-273.

Rubin, Z., Hill, C. T., Peplau, L. A., & Dunkel-Schetter, C. (1980). Self-disclosure in dating couples: Sex roles and the ethic of openness. *Journal of Marriage and the Family, 42,* 305-317.

Russell, D. H. (1982). *Rape in marriage.* New York: Macmillan.

Russell, D. H. (1984). *Sexual exploitation.* Beverly Hills, CA: Sage.

Russell, D. H. (1990). *Rape in marriage* (expanded edition). Bloomington: Indiana University Press.

Saal, F. E., Johnson, C. B., & Weber, N. (1989). Friendly or sexy? It may depend on whom you ask. *Psychology of Women Quarterly, 13,* 263-276.

Safilios-Rothschild, C. (1976). A macro- and micro-examination of family power and love: An exchange model. *Journal of Marriage and the Family, 38,* 355-362.

Scanzoni, J., Polonko, K., Teachman, J., & Thompson, L. (1989). *The sexual bond: Rethinking families and close relationships.* Newbury Park, CA: Sage.

Schaefer, M. T., & Olson, D. H. (1981). Assessing intimacy: The PAIR inventory. *Journal of Marital and Family Therapy, 7,* 47-60.

Schenk, J., Pfrang, H., & Rausche, A. (1983). Personality traits versus the quality of the marital relationship as the determinant of marital sexuality. *Archives of Sexual Behavior, 12,* 31-42.

Schilit, R., Lie, G. L., & Montagne, M. (1990). Substance abuse as a correlate of violence in intimate lesbian relationships. *Journal of Homosexuality, 19,* 51-65.

Schwartz, P. (1992). Who informs the public about close relationships? *Bulletin for the International Society for the Study of Personal Relationships, 8,* 1-3.

Seltzer, R. (1992). The social location of those holding antihomosexual attitudes. *Sex Roles, 26,* 391-398.

Shapurian, R., & Hojat, M. (1985). Sexual and premarital attitudes of Iranian college students. *Psychological Reports, 57,* 67-74.

Sherwin, R., & Corbett, S. (1985). Campus sexual norms and dating relationships: A trend analysis. *Journal of Sex Research, 21,* 258-274.

Shotland, R. L. (1989). A model of the causes of date rape in developing and close relationships. In C. Hendrick (Ed.), *Close relationships* (pp. 247-270). Newbury Park, CA: Sage.

Shotland, R. L., & Craig, J. M. (1988). Can men and women differentiate between friendly and sexually interested behavior? *Social Psychology Quarterly, 51,* 66-73.

Shotland, R. L., & Goodstein, L. (1983). Just because she doesn't want to doesn't mean it's rape: An experimentally based causal model of the perception of rape in a dating situation. *Social Psychology Quarterly, 46,* 220-232.

Sigal, J., Gibbs, M., Adams, B., & Derfler, R. (1988). The effect of romantic and nonromantic films on perception of female friendly and seductive behavior. *Sex Roles, 19,* 545-554.

Simenauer, J., & Carroll, D. (1982). *Singles: The new Americans.* New York: Simon & Schuster.

Simpson, J. A. (1987). The dissolution of romantic relationships: Factors involved in relationship stability and emotional distress. *Journal of Personality and Social Psychology, 53,* 683-692.

Simpson, J. A., & Gangestad, S. W. (1991). Individual differences in sociosexuality: Evidence for convergent and discriminant validity. *Journal of Personality and Social Psychology, 60,* 870-883.

Simpson, J. A., Gangestad, S. W., & Lerma, M. (1990). Perception of physical attractiveness: Mechanisms involved in the maintenance of romantic relationships. *Journal of Personality and Social Psychology, 59,* 1192-1201.

Singh, B. K. (1980). Trends in attitudes toward premarital sexual relations. *Journal of Marriage and the Family, 42,* 387-393.

Singh, B. K., Walton, B. L., & Williams, J. S. (1976). Extramarital sexual permissiveness: Conditions and contingencies. *Journal of Marriage and the Family, 38,* 701-712.

Smith, A. D., Resick, P. A., & Kilpatrick, D. G. (1980). Relationships among gender, sex-role attitudes, sexual attitudes, thoughts, and behaviors. *Psychological Reports, 46,* 359-367.

Snyder, D. K. (1979). Multidimensional assessment of marital satisfaction. *Journal of Marriage and the Family, 41,* 813-823.

Snyder, D. K. (1981). *Manual for the Marital Satisfaction Inventory.* Los Angeles: Western Psychological Services.

Snyder, M., Berscheid, E., & Glick, P. (1985). Focusing on the exterior and the interior: Two investigations of the initiation of personal relationships. *Journal of Personality and Social Psychology, 48,* 1427-1439.

Snyder, M., Simpson, J. A., & Gangestad, S. (1986). Personality and sexual relations. *Journal of Personality and Social Psychology, 51,* 181-190.

Spanier, G. B., & Margolies, R. L. (1983). Marital separation and extramarital sexual behavior. *Journal of Sex Research, 19,* 23-48.

Sponaugle, G. C. (1989). Attitudes toward extramarital relations. In K. McKinney & S. Sprecher (Eds.), *Human sexuality: The societal and interpersonal context* (pp. 187-209). Norwood, NJ: Ablex.

Sprague, J., & Quadagno, D. (1989). Gender and sexual motivation: An exploration of two assumptions. *Journal of Psychology and Human Sexuality, 2,* 57-76.

Spreadbury, C. L. (1982). The "permissiveness with affection" norm and the labeling of deviants. *Personnel and Guidance Journal, 60,* 280-282.

Sprecher, S. (1986). [How couples come to meet and begin dating]. Unpublished data.

Sprecher, S. (1989a). The importance to males and females of physical attractiveness, earning potential, and expressiveness in initial attraction. *Sex Roles, 21,* 591-607.

Sprecher, S. (1989b). Premarital sexual standards for different categories of individuals. *Journal of Sex Research, 26,* 232-248.

Sprecher, S. (1991). The impact of the threat of AIDS on heterosexual dating relationships. *Journal of Psychology and Human Sexuality, 3,* 3-23.

Sprecher, S., & McKinney, K. (1987). Barriers in the initiation of intimate heterosexual relationships and strategies for intervention. In H. Gochros & W. Ricketts (Eds.), *Social work and love* (pp. 97-110). New York: Haworth.

Sprecher, S., McKinney, K., & Orbuch, T. L. (1987). Has the double standard disappeared?: An experimental test. *Social Psychology Quarterly, 50,* 24-31.

Sprecher, S., McKinney, K., & Orbuch, T. L. (1991). The effect of current sexual behavior on friendship, dating, and marriage desirability. *Journal of Sex Research, 28,* 387-408.

Sprecher, S., McKinney, K., Walsh, R., & Anderson, C. (1988). A revision of the Reiss Premarital Sexual Permissiveness Scale. *Journal of Marriage and the Family, 50,* 821-828.

Sprecher, S., Hatfield, E., Potapova, E., Levitskaya, A., & Cortese, A. (1992). *Sexual miscommunication: Saying no when meaning yes and saying yes when meaning no.* Manuscript submitted for publication.

Stafford, L., & Canary, D. J. (1991). Maintenance strategies and romantic relationship type, gender and relational characteristics. *Journal of Social and Personal Relationships, 8,* 217-242.

Staples, R. E. (1978). *The black woman in America.* Chicago: Nelson-Hall.

Struckman-Johnson, C. (1988). Forced sex on dates: It happens to men too. *Journal of Sex Research, 24,* 234-241.

Struckman-Johnson, D., & Struckman-Johnson, C. (1991). Men and women's acceptance of coercive sexual strategies varied by initiator gender and couple intimacy. *Sex Roles, 25,* 661-676.

Surra, C. A. (1990). Research and theory on mate selection and premarital relationships in the 1980s. *Journal of Marriage and the Family, 52,* 844-865.

Sweet, E. (1985, October). Date rape: The story of an epidemic and those who deny it. *MS,* pp. 56-59, 84-85.

Sweet, J. A., Bumpass, L. L., & Call, V. R. A. (1988). *NSFH codebook and documentation: Self-administered questionnaire.* Madison: University of Wisconsin, Center for Demography and Ecology.

Symons, D. (1979). *The evolution of human sexuality.* New York: Oxford University Press.

Tavris, C., & Sadd, S. (1977). *The Redbook report of female sexuality.* New York: Dell.

Terman, L. M., Buttenweiser, P., Ferguson, L. W., Johnson, W. B., & Wilson, D. P. (1938). *Psychological factors in marital happiness.* New York: McGraw-Hill.

Tesch, S. A. (1985). The Psychosocial Intimacy Questionnaire: Validational studies and an investigation of sex roles. *Journal of Social and Personal Relationships, 2,* 471-488.

Testa, R. J., Kinder, B. N., & Ironson, G. (1987). Heterosexual bias in the perception of loving relationships of gay males and lesbians. *Journal of Sex Research, 23,* 163-172.

Thompson, A. P. (1983). Extramarital sex: A review of the research literature. *Journal of Sex Research, 19,* 1-22.

Townsend, J. M., & Levy, G. D. (1990). Effects of potential partners' physical attractiveness and socioeconomic status on sexuality and partner selection. *Archives of Sexual Behavior, 19,* 149-164.

Traupmann, J., Hatfield, E., & Wexler, P. (1983). Equity and sexual satisfaction in dating couples. *British Journal of Social Psychology, 22,* 33-40.

Trussell, J., & Westoff, C. F. (1980). Contraceptive practice and trends in coital frequency. *Family Planning Perspectives, 12,* 246-249.

Udry, J. R. (1980). Changes in the frequency of marital intercourse from panel data. *Archives of Sexual Behavior, 9,* 319-325.

Udry, J. R., Deven, F. R., & Coleman, S. J. (1982). A cross-national comparison of the relative influence of male and female age on the frequency of marital intercourse. *Journal of Biosocial Science, 14,* 1-6.

Udry, J. R., & Eckland, B. K. (1982, September). *The benefits of being attractive: Differential payoffs for men and women.* Paper presented at the American Sociological Association, San Francisco, CA.

Udry, J. R., & Morris, N. M. (1978). Relative contribution of male and female age to the frequency of marital intercourse. *Social Biology, 25,* 128-134.

Vance, E. B., & Wagner, N. N. (1976). Written descriptions of orgasm: A study of sex differences. *Archives of Sexual Behavior, 5,* 87-98.

Voeller, B. (1991). AIDS and heterosexual anal intercourse. *Archives of Sexual Behavior, 20,* 233-276.

Walsh, R. (1989). Premarital sex among teenagers and young adults. In K. McKinney & S. Sprecher (Eds.), *Human sexuality: The societal and interpersonal context* (pp. 162-186). Norwood, NJ: Ablex.

Walster (Hatfield), E. (1965). The effect of self-esteem on romantic liking. *Journal of Experimental Social Psychology, 1,* 184-197.

Walster (Hatfield), E., Aronson, V., Abrahams, D., & Rottman, L. (1966). The importance of physical attractiveness in dating behavior. *Journal of Personality and Social Psychology, 4,* 508-516.

Walster (Hatfield), E., Traupmann, J., & Walster, G. W. (1978). Equity and extramarital sexuality. *Archives of Sexual Behavior, 7,* 127-141.

Walster (Hatfield), E., Walster, G. W., & Berscheid, E. (1978). *Equity: Theory and research.* Boston: Allyn & Bacon.

Walster (Hatfield), E., Walster, G. W., & Traupmann, J. (1978). Equity and premarital sex. *Journal of Personality and Social Psychology, 36,* 82-92.

Ward, S. K., Chapman, K., Cohn, E., White, S., & Williams, K. (1991). Acquaintance rape and the college social scene. *Family Relations, 40,* 65-71.

Waring, E. M., McElrath, D., Lefcoe, D., & Weisz, D. (1981). Dimensions of intimacy in marriage. *Psychiatry, 44,* 169-175.

Waring, E. M., Tillman, M. P., Frelick, L., Russell, L., & Weisz, G. (1980). Concepts of intimacy in the general population. *Journal of Nervous and Mental Disease, 168,* 471-474.

Warshaw, R. (1988). *I never called it rape.* New York: Harper & Row.

Warshaw, R., & Parrot, A. (1991). The contribution of sex-role socialization to acquaintance rape. In A. Parrot & L. Bechhofer (Eds.), *Acquaintance rape: The hidden crime* (pp. 73-82). New York: John Wiley.

Waterman, C. K., Chiauzzi, E., & Gruenbaum, M. (1979). The relationship between enjoyment and actualization of self and sexual partner. *Journal of Sex Research, 15,* 253-263.

Waterman, C. K., Dawson, L. J., & Bologna, M. J. (1989). Sexual coercion in gay male and lesbian relationships: Predictions and implications for support services. *Journal of Sex Research, 26,* 118-124.

Weinberg, M. S., Swensson, R. G., & Hammersmith, S. K. (1983). Sexual autonomy and the status of women: Models of female sexuality in U.S. sex manuals from 1950-1980. *Social Problems, 30,* 312-324.

Weinberg, M. S., & Williams, C. J. (1988). Black sexuality: A test of two theories. *Journal of Sex Research, 25,* 197-218.

Weis, D. L., Slosnerick, M., Cate, R., & Sollie, D. L. (1986). A survey instrument for assessing the cognitive association of sex, love, and marriage. *Journal of Sex Research, 22,* 206-220.

Weiss, R. S. (1969). The fund of sociability. *Transaction, 7,* 36-43.

Weiss, R. S. (1973). *Loneliness.* Cambridge, MA: MIT Press.

Wells, J. W. (1990). The sexual vocabularies of heterosexual and homosexual males and females for communicating erotically with a sexual partner. *Archives of Sexual Behavior, 19,* 139-147.

Werebe, M. J. G., & Reinert, M. (1983). Attitudes of French students toward sexuality. *Journal of Adolescence, 6,* 145-159.

Westoff, C. F. (1974). Coital frequency and contraception. *Family Planning Perspectives, 6,* 136-141.

Wheeless, L. R., Wheeless, V. E., & Baus, R. (1984). Sexual communication, communication satisfaction, and solidarity in the developmental stages of intimate relationships. *Western Journal of Speech Communication, 48,* 217-230.

White, J. W., & Humphrey, J. A. (1991). Young people's attitudes toward acquaintance rape. In A. Parrot & L. Bechhofer (Eds.), *Acquaintance rape: The hidden crime* (pp. 43-56). New York: John Wiley.

Whitley, B. E. (1988, August). *College students' reasons for sexual intercourse: A sex role perspective.* Paper presented at the 96th Annual Meeting of the American Psychological Association, Atlanta, GA.

Wiersma, G. E. (1983). *Cohabitation, an alternative to marriage? A cross-cultural study.* Boston: Martinus Nijhoff.

Williams, J. D., & Jacoby, A. P. (1989). The effects of premarital heterosexual and homosexual experience on dating and marriage desirability. *Journal of Marriage and the Family, 51,* 489-497.

Woll, S. (1986). So many to choose from: Decision strategies in videodating. *Journal of Social and Personal Relationships, 3,* 43-53.

Woll, S., & Cozby, P. (1987). Videodating and other alternatives to traditional methods of relationship initiation. In W. Jones & D. Perlman (Eds.), *Advances in personal relationships* (Vol. 1, pp. 69-109). Greenwich, CT: JAI.

Yalom, M., Brewster, W., & Estler, S. (1981). Women of the fifties: Their past sexual experiences and current sexual attitudes in the context of mother/daughter relationships. *Sex Roles, 7,* 877-887.

Zimmerman, R., Sprecher, S., Langer, L. M., & Holloway, C. D. (1992). *Which adolescents can't say "no" to unwanted sex in a dating relationship?* Manuscript submitted for publication.

Index

About the Authors

Susan Sprecher is Professor of Sociology and Anthropology at Illinois State University at Normal. She received her Ph.D. in sociology (with a social psychology concentration) from the University of Wisconsin in 1985. She has conducted research and written primarily in the field of close relationships but also has done work in the area of sexuality and the interface between the two areas. Her articles and chapters have been on a variety of topics, including sexual attitudes, premarital relationship breakups, emotions, love, the role of physical attractiveness in attraction, equity and exchange, and the initiation of relationships. She is active in organizations on close or personal relationships, including serving as Editor (1988-1992) of *Bulletin for the International Society of the Study of Personal Relationships* and on the editorial boards of *Journal of Social and Personal Relationships* and *Journal of Sex Research.*

Kathleen McKinney obtained her Ph.D. from the University of Wisconsin at Madison in 1982. Her major field is sociology, with a minor in social psychology. She has taught at Oklahoma State University and is currently Professor of Sociology at Illinois State University at Normal. She has written several journal articles and a book chapter on sexual harassment in academia. Currently she is involved in an interview study of faculty at three institutions, discussing their experiences with sexual harassment. Other areas of research include sexual standards and contraceptive attitudes. She also co-edited *Human Sexuality: The Societal and Interpersonal Context* (Ablex, 1989) and *Sexuality in Close Relationships* (Lawrence Erlbaum, 1991) with Susan Sprecher. She is concerned with the quality of teaching and publishes in *Teaching Sociology,* and serves as Director of the University Teaching Workshop at ISU, and as a member of the ASA Teaching Resources Group.